Editor
Kim Fields

Managing Editors
Karen J. Goldfluss, M.S. Ed.
Ina Massler Levin, M.A.

Editorial Project Manager
Mara Ellen Guckian

Illustrator
Kelly McMahon

Cover Artist
Barb Lorseyedi

Art Manager
Kevin Barnes

Art Director
CJae Froshay

Imaging
Rosa C. See

Publisher
Mary D. Smith, M.S. Ed.

Grades Pre-K-1

A Poem In My Pocket
Spring

Author

Traci Ferguson Geiser, M.A.

Teacher Created Resources, Inc.
6421 Industry Way
Westminster, CA 92683
www.teachercreated.com
ISBN-1-4206-3142-x
©2005 Teacher Created Resources, Inc.
Made in U.S.A.

Table of Contents

Introduction

A Poem in My Pocket: Spring was designed to offer busy teachers hassle-free, developmentally appropriate literacy experiences for young children. All of the activities included in this book will help students develop prereading skills and give children fun, hands-on experiences with print. Phonological awareness skills, such as rhyming, syllabication, and beginning and ending sounds, will be focused on throughout the lessons. Students will review lines of poetry, observing sentences and punctuation. Further, they will have opportunities to point out the words forming each sentence and note the syllables (and phonemes) used to make different words.

The Poem in My Pocket series consists of three seasonally themed books: *Fall, Winter,* and *Spring.* The books include five units, each containing a full week of thematic lesson plans based on an original poem. The *Spring* book incorporates the following topics: Plants and Seeds, Farm Animals, Picnics, Bugs, and Frogs.

Each unit includes the following components:

Original Poem: Each poem in the book was created to enhance the topics typically explored in preschool and kindergarten. Each poem can be enlarged to display in the classroom or copied to create a book of poetry for your classroom library. These simple poems will complement existing curriculum and help build oral language skills. Reproducible Pocket Chart Cards and Picture Cards are included for each poem and require minimal teacher preparation.

Daily Interactive Pocket Chart Activities: Using the poem text, students will participate in hands-on games and activities that will promote prereading skills, including phonological awareness. Lesson plans for each day focus on essential emergent literacy skills including letter and sound recognition, rhyming, syllabication, basic sight words, and basic punctuation.

Home/School Connection: The week's activities culminate with a fun Home/School Connection activity. A letter pertaining to the weekly theme is included to copy and send home to parents and caregivers. This letter invites parents to take an active role in their children's learning by assisting in a prereading activity, thus fostering literacy development. This letter will encourage parent involvement and extend learning into the home.

Student Poem Page: A page containing the unit's poem, with ample room for children's illustrations, is included. Use this page to help develop fine motor skills, left-to-right correspondence, and oral language.

Mini Book: The Mini Book for each poem gives children interactive practice with books and book parts such as reading from front-to-back, left-to-right, and top-to-bottom. The end of each Mini Book contains a simple activity that will give children the opportunity to interact with the poem's text.

Literature Links: A list of related children's literature is included to complement the unit, and help generate and retain interest in the unit's theme.

How to Use This Book

Before you begin each lesson, you will need to gather some supplies. A basic pocket chart with ten pockets will be needed to hold the Pocket Chart Cards. Pocket charts are available at most teacher supply stores and will be an asset to your early childhood classroom by giving your students many opportunities to interact with print. You may also wish to invest in a pocket chart stand to provide quick, rollaway storage for your pocket chart. You will need a few basic supplies to prepare and complete each lesson, including scissors, crayons, a stapler, tape, and markers.

Prior to starting each unit, you will need to prepare each of the following:

1. Reproduce the Home/School Connection Letter for each student. Go over the activity with your class before sending it home to be sure they understand what they are being asked to do with their parents. You may want to offer a special reward (sticker or small toy) for children who complete the activity.

2. Cut out the Pocket Chart Cards and Picture Cards for the unit. You may want to laminate the cards or attach them to tagboard for durability since all of the activities are hands-on and the cards will be handled a great deal. You can color the Picture Cards if you wish; just be certain to read the entire unit first to determine if there are any special color requirements for the pictures. Arranging the cards in the correct order and storing them in a large envelope or resealable, plastic bag will help with the organization and management of each poem. Commercial sentence strip file boxes can also be purchased at your local teacher supply store.

3. Reproduce and assemble a poem Mini Book for each student. Copy the pages, cut them out, and put them in order. Staple the pages on the left-hand side to create a small book version of the poem for each child to take home. Encourage the children to read their books to their families and friends at home.

4. Reproduce the Student Poem Page for each child. After the child has illustrated the page, hold on to it. Once several units are complete, you may want to compile these individual pages into a booklet for each child to take home periodically and read to their families. Using an inexpensive folder for three-hole-punched paper will allow you to add additional poems to the booklets as you complete them.

   Make a mini pointer for the poem collection folder. Attach a 12" string or piece of yarn to one end of a craft stick. Tie the other end of the string or yarn to a ring in the folder. Children can use the pointer to point to the words as they read each poem.

   At the end of the year, give each child a large sheet of folded construction paper to decorate and use as a cover. Staple to poems inside. Save the original mini-binders to use again next year.

5. You may wish to find the Literature Links or other books on the theme in your school or neighborhood library. Reading these books will help generate interest and extend the knowledge the children gain from the unit. Keep the books in an accessible place in the reading area once they have been introduced.

   Optional: Each unit begins with a full-page copy of the poem. These pages can be enlarged, colored, and displayed in the classroom. Another option is to copy the pages and create a book for the class library once all the poems have been shared.

Plants and Seeds

Plant some seeds in a row.

An alphabet you will grow.

Start with A and go to Z.

Yummy veggies you will see.

Pick a letter, say its name.

Put them in order, play the game.

Plants and Seeds

Unit Preparation

Copy and send home the Plants and Seeds Home/School Connection Parent Letter and Homework Page (pages 8–9). Copy and cut apart the Plants and Seeds Pocket Chart Cards (pages 10–16). Copy, color, and cut out the Plants and Seeds Picture Cards (pages 17–18). Place all the cards in the pocket chart in the correct places. Copy the Plants and Seeds Student Poem Page (page 19) and the *Plants and Seeds* Mini Book (pages 20–23) for each child. Copy, color, and cut out the Veggie Cards (pages 24–26). See page 4 for additional preparation tips.

Student Poem Page

Have a discussion about vegetables and seeds. Ask children to name different vegetables they know. Then ask them if they know how vegetables grow. (How do vegetables start out? Where do they grow? What do they need to grow?) Then direct the children to illustrate their Plants and Seeds Student Poem Page by drawing a garden full of veggies. Ask each student to write the beginning letter for the veggie he or she has drawn next to the picture, or write it for him or her. Ask the child to fill in the bottom of the page with a vegetable name on the first blank line and its beginning letter on the second blank line.

Mini Book

Assemble a *Plants and Seeds* Mini Book for each child. Have the children color the pages and read their Mini Books to others. At the end of the week, invite each child to take the book home and read it to his or her family.

Literature Links

Eating the Alphabet by Lois Ehlert (Red Wagon Books, 1996)

From Seed to Plant by Gail Gibbons (Holiday House, Reprint edition, 1993)

Growing Vegetable Soup by Lois Ehlert (Voyager Books, Reprint edition, 1990)

How a Seed Grows by Helene J. Jordan (Harper Trophy, Revised edition, 1992)

The Tiny Seed by Eric Carle (Aladdin, Reprint edition, 2001)

Pocket Chart Activities

Monday: Introduce the Poem

Ask the children if they have ever planted seeds. Ask them to tell what types they planted. Ask the children if they know with what letter the type of seed starts and share it with the class. Read the poem, "Plants and Seeds," aloud to the children. Reread the poem, pointing to the words as you go. Invite the children to read the poem aloud with you.

Tuesday: Phoneme Substitution

In Phoneme Substitution, children substitute one phoneme for another to create new words. For example,

> **Teacher:** The word is cat. Change the /c/ to /m/. What is the new word?

> **Children:** *mat.*

Use the following words from the poem to practice phoneme substitution as outlined above:

> *name*—replace the /n/ with /c/, /f/, /g/, /s/, /t/

> *yummy*—replace the initial /y/ with /g/, /m/, /r/, /t/

> *row*—replace the /r/ with /b/, /l/, /m/, /s/, /t/

Wednesday: Order in the Garden

Ask the children to sit on the floor in a circle. Spread out the Veggie Cards (pages 24–26) in the middle of the circle. Read the poem together to introduce the game. Beginning with the letter **A**, ask a child to find the card in the middle of the circle, say its name, and then place it on the floor at one side of the circle. Next, have a student find the letter **B** and place it next to the **A** card. Continue to make a straight line across the middle of the circle by adding each letter in alphabetical order.

Thursday: I See

Read the poem aloud together. Tell the children that you would like them to listen to the following words to see if they can hear a sound that is the same in both words: *see, seeds.* Tell the children that the long /e/ sound is found in both words. Ask a child to come up and find the word *see* in the pocket chart. Hold up the card for the class to see and say each letter in the word together. Ask another child to come up and find the word *seeds* in the pocket chart. Hold up the card for the class to see and say each letter in the word together. Hold up both cards together and ask the children which two letters they think make up the sound of long /e/ in these words. Explain to the class that when they see two **e**'s together in a word, it makes the sound of long /e/.

Friday: Culminating Activity

Invite the children to bring their Homework Page to circle time. Go through each word family (-at, -ig, -ug), having the children read each word they created for each family to check for accuracy. Reread the poem together one final time.

Plants and Seeds

Plant some seeds in a row.
An alphabet you will grow.
Start with A and go to Z.
Yummy veggies you will see.
Pick a letter, say its name.
Put them in order, play the game.

Hello,

This week we will be learning this poem about plants and seeds. Please read the poem with your child to help him or her learn it. Using the poem as a springboard, we will work with alphabetical order, replace sounds in words with different sounds to form new words (phoneme substitution), and focus on the long /e/ sound.

Please help your child complete the activity on the Homework Page to practice phoneme substitution. Ask your child to cut out the letter cards at the bottom of the page. Spread out the letter cards on the table or floor and ask your child to choose a card, then place it over a box as the beginning letter of a word. Sound out the word and determine whether it is a real word. If it is a word, attach the card to the page with tape or glue. If it is not a word, continue putting it in each row until a real word is formed. Continue until all of the blanks are filled with new letters. Next, help your child write the words on the lines under each box. Please send the homework to school on

_____.

Your child will be bringing home a *Plants and Seeds* Mini Book of the poem this week. Please ask him or her to read it to you. Your child may also want to read it to a special friend or relative.

I can't wait to "see" what words you create together!

Sincerely,

_____

Homework Page.

Directions: Cut out the letter cards at the bottom of the page. Spread them out on the table or floor. Have your child choose a card. Place it over a box as the beginning letter of a word. If it makes a real word, tape or glue the card to the page. If it is not a word, continue trying until a new word is formed. Fill all the blanks with letters.

Write the words on the lines under the boxes.

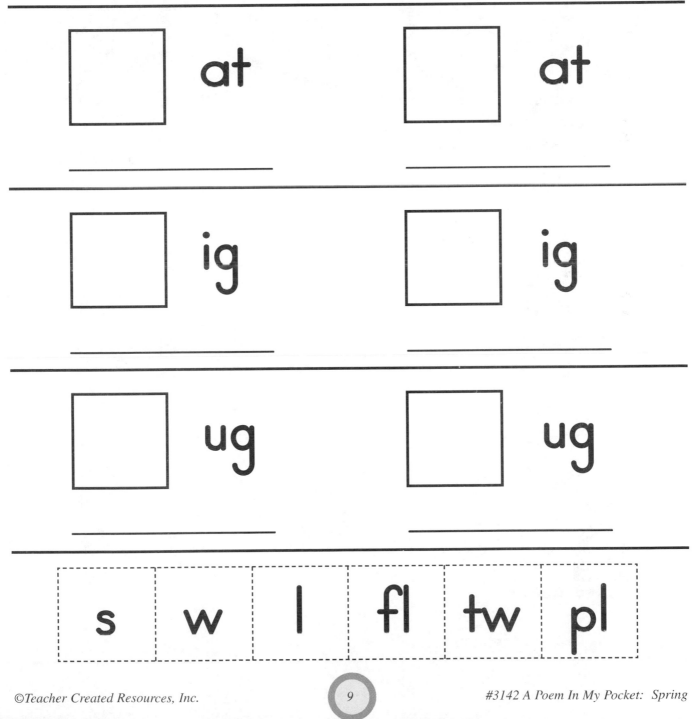

at

at

ig

ig

ug

ug

s   w   l   fl   tw   pl

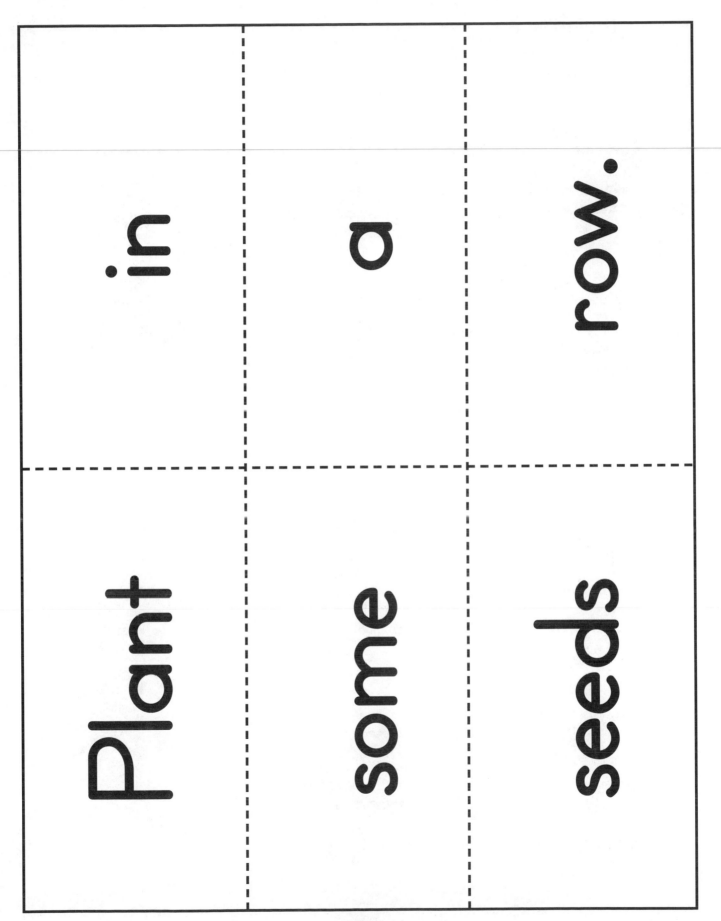

Plant

some

seeds

in

a

row.

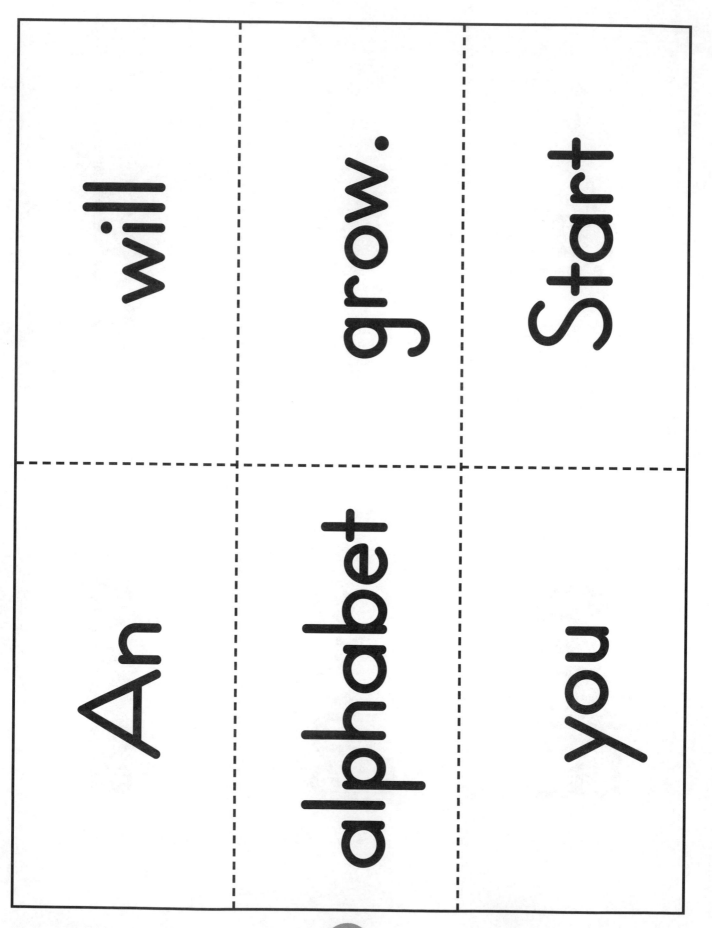

will

grow.

Start

An

alphabet

you

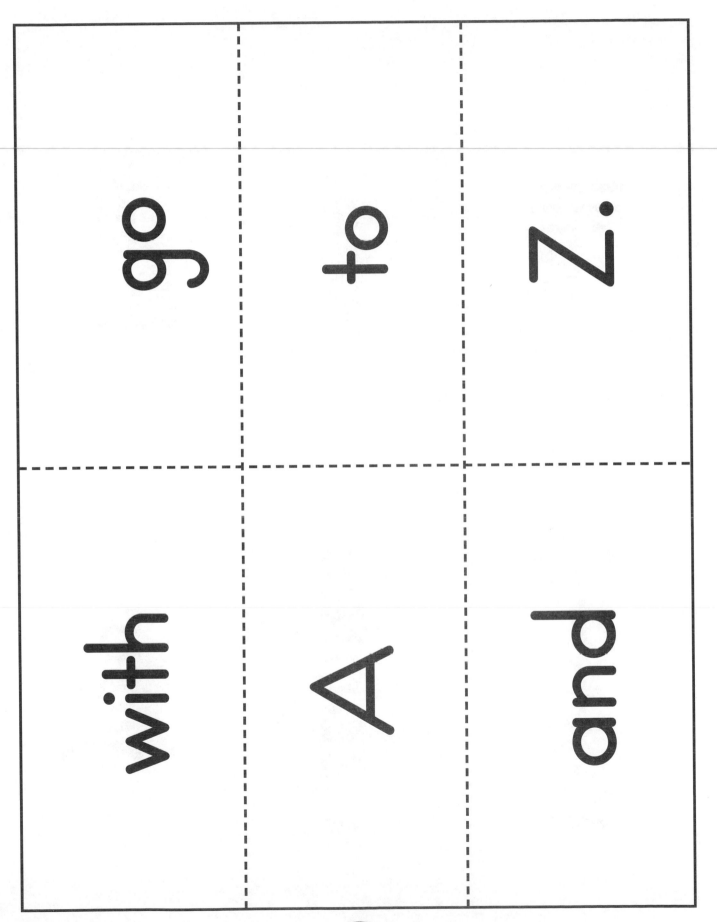

go

to

z.

with

A

and

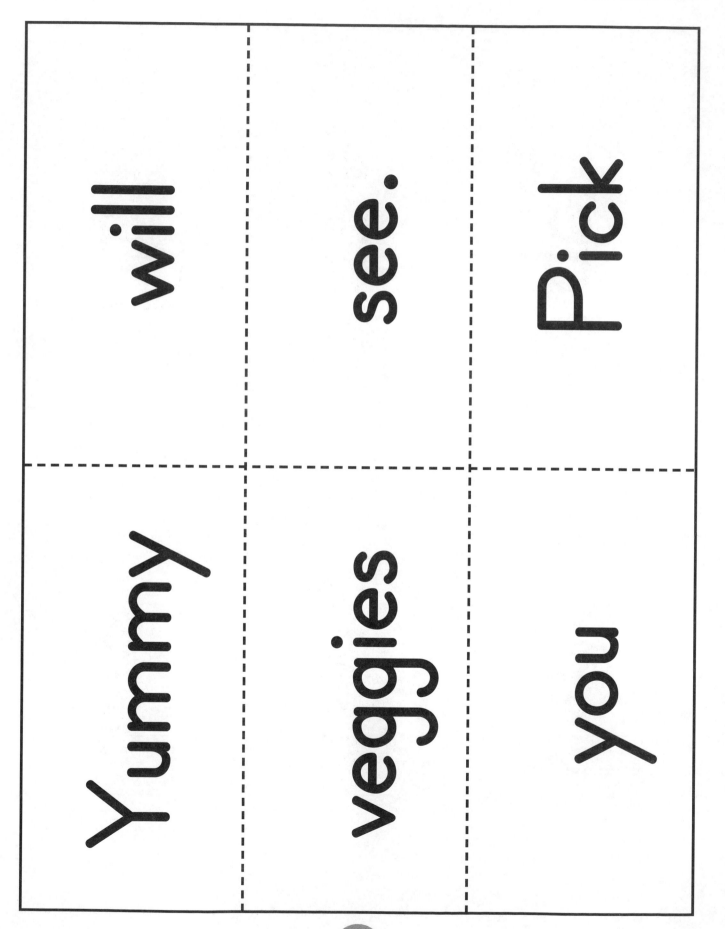

will

see.

Pick

Yummy

veggies

you

its

name.

Put

a

letter,

say

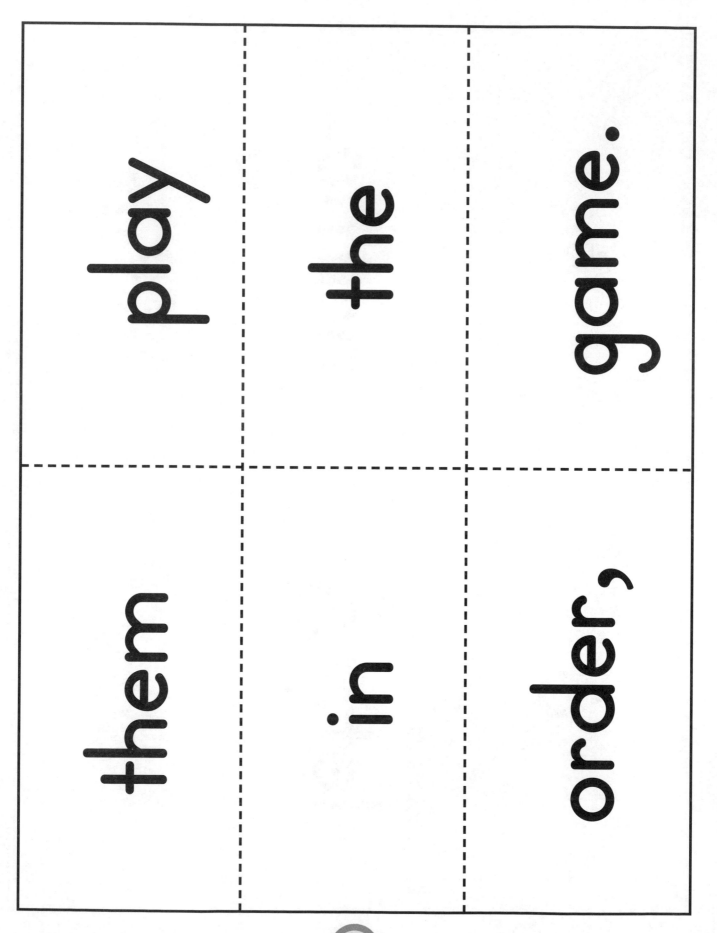

play

the

game.

them

in

order,

2

3

Aa Bb Cc Dd Ee Ff Gg Hh Ii Jj Kk

Ll Mm Nn Oo Pp Qq Rr

Ss Tt Uu Vv Ww Xx Yy Zz

1

Plants and Seeds

Plant some seeds in a row.

An alphabet you will grow.

Start with A and go to Z.

Yummy veggies you will see.

Pick a letter, say its name.

Put them in order, play the game.

_____ begins with the letter _____ .

Plant some seeds in a row.

1

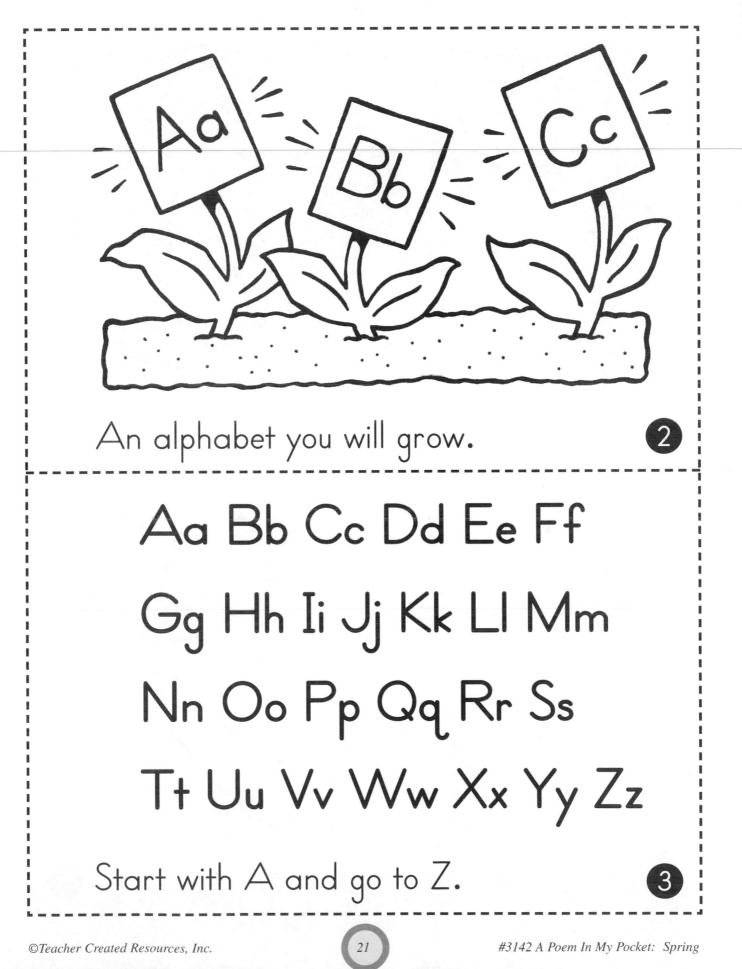

An alphabet you will grow. **2**

Aa Bb Cc Dd Ee Ff

Gg Hh Ii Jj Kk Ll Mm

Nn Oo Pp Qq Rr Ss

Tt Uu Vv Ww Xx Yy Zz

Start with A and go to Z. **3**

Yummy veggies you will see. **4**

Pick a letter, say its name. **5**

Put them in order, play the game. **6**

Circle the letters **"ee"** in the text.
Write a word with **ee** in it. _____ **7**

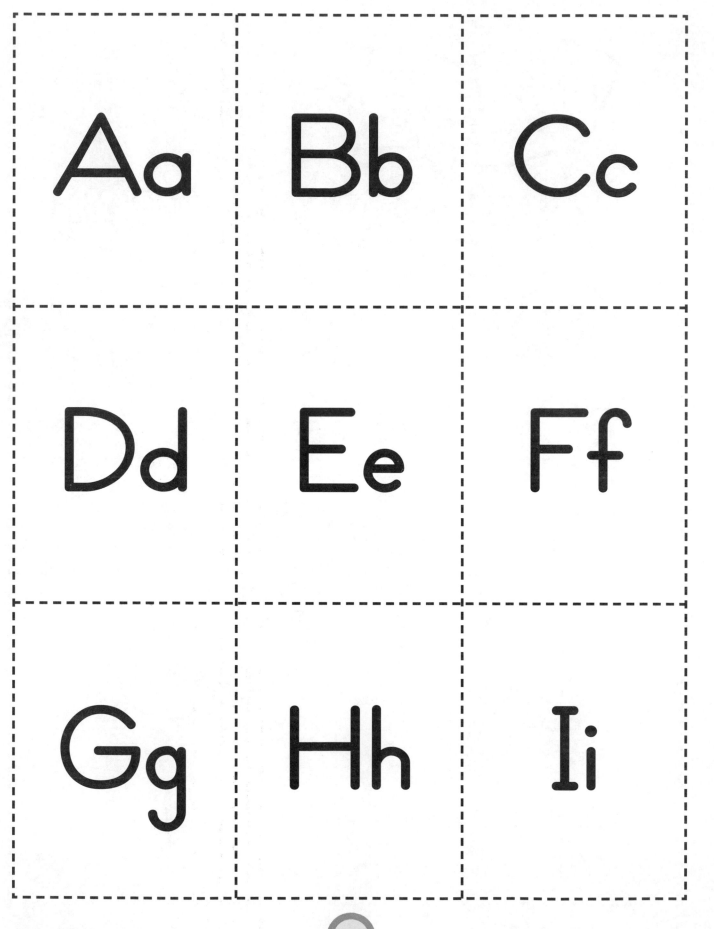

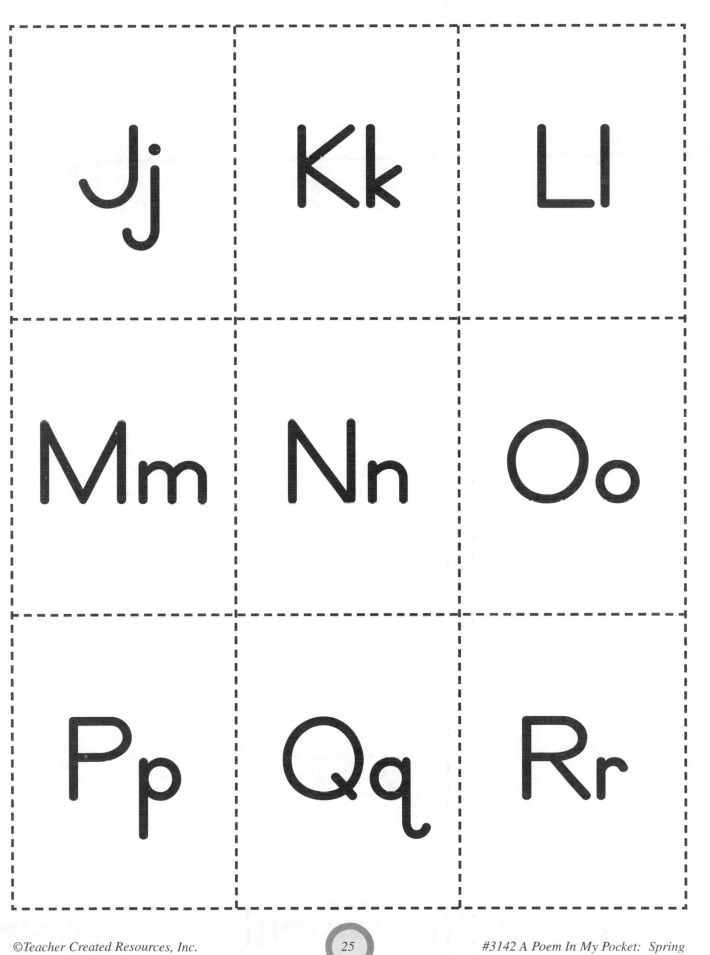

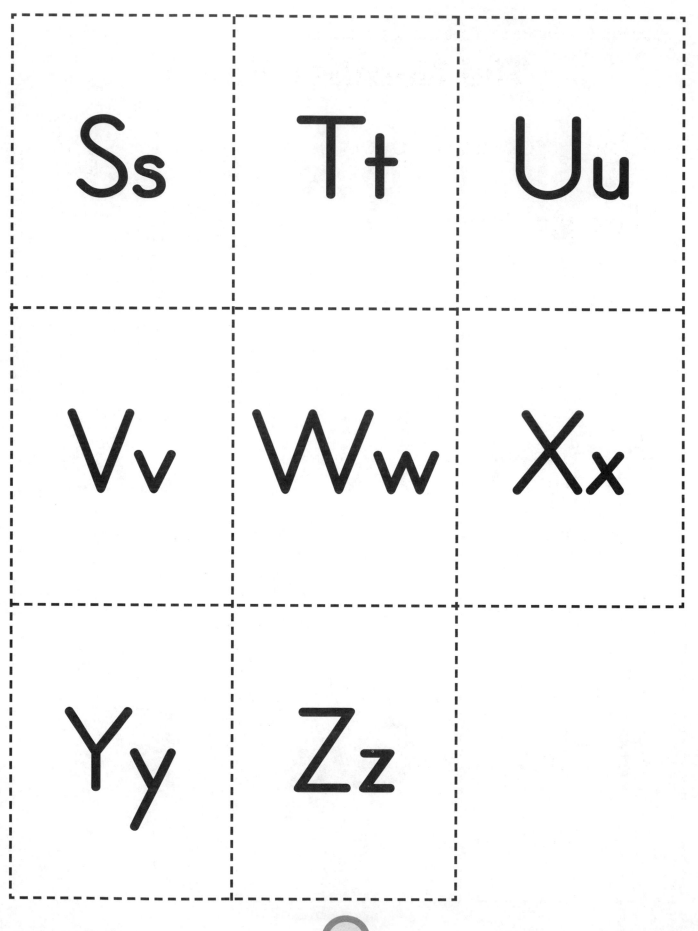

The Number Farm

One chick says "peep."

Two pigs sleep.

Three horses neigh.

Four donkeys bray.

Five puppies chew.

Six cows say "moo."

Seven goats snack.

Eight ducks say "quack."

Nine sheep have fun.

Ten kittens run.

Farm Animals

Unit Preparation

Copy and send home the Farm Animals Home/School Connection Parent Letter and Homework Pages (pages 30–32). Copy and cut apart the Farm Animals Pocket Chart Cards and Number Cards (pages 33–40). Copy, color, and cut out the Farm Animals Picture Cards (pages 41–43). Place all the cards in the pocket chart in the correct places. Copy the Farm Animals Student Poem Page (page 44) and *The Number Farm* Mini Book (pages 45–50) for each child. See page 4 for additional preparation tips.

Student Poem Page

Ask children if they have ever visited a farm. What kinds of things did they see? What animals lived on the farm? What did they hear? What sound did each animal make? Then direct students to choose their favorite line from the poem. Ask them to copy those words on the line at the bottom of the Farm Animals Student Poem Page. Next, ask them to illustrate this line of the poem by drawing the correct number of animals performing the action indicated.

Mini Book

Assemble *The Number Farm* Mini Book for each child. Have the children color the pages and read their Mini Books to others. At the end of the week, invite each child to take the Mini Book home and read it to his or her family.

Literature Links

Barnyard Banter by Denise Fleming (Henry Holt and Co., Reprint edition, 1997)

Big Red Barn by Margaret Wise Brown (Scholastic, 1989)

The Day The Goose Got Loose by Reeve Lindbergh (Puffin Books, 1995)

Inside a Barn in the Country by Alyssa Satin Capucilli (Scholastic, 1995)

Not Now Said the Cow by Joanne Oppenheim (Bank Street, 1981)

Pocket Chart Activities

Monday: Introduce the Poem

Ask each child to name his or her favorite farm animal. Read the poem, "The Number Farm," aloud to the children. Reread the poem, pointing to the words as you go. Invite the children to read the poem aloud with you.

Tuesday: Name That Number

Read the poem with the class. Remove the number word from each line of the poem, mix the word cards up, and hand them out to the class. Reread the poem, stopping at the place where each number word belongs. After the class has determined which number word belongs in the space, ask the children to look at their cards to determine whether they have the missing card. You may help by giving them cues to look at the beginning letter and sound of each word. Continue until the poem is reassembled, then reread the poem together. If your class is not yet ready to use number words, you may wish to use the number cards (pages 39–40) in place of the number words.

Wednesday: Pigs or Piggies

Draw a two column chart on the board or chart paper. Tell the children that you would like them to help you fill in the chart with the animal names we use when we are talking about one animal and more than one animal (singular and plural words). Write the word *One* on top of the left-hand column and the phrase *More Than One* on top of the right-hand column. Ask a volunteer to come up and read the name of the first animal in the poem. Help him or her determine if the animal is singular or plural and write the word in the correct column. In the first line, *chick* is singular and would be written in the column titled "One." Next, ask the class how you would use the animal name if you said, "On the farm, I saw two _____." Have a volunteer come up and write the word *chicks* in the column labeled "More Than One." Draw attention to the plural word that ends in **s**. Continue in this fashion until you have listed the singular and plural forms of each animal name on the chart. (**Note:** You will need to explain that endings sometimes change before adding a plural **s**, as in *puppies*. Also note that the singular and plural words for *sheep* are the same.)

Thursday: Phoneme Identity

In Phoneme Identity, children can recognize the same sounds in different words. For example,

Teacher: What sound is the same in *bat, ball,* and *boy*? **Students:** The first sound, /b/, is the same.

Use the following sets of words from the poem to practice phoneme identity (**p**uppies, **p**igs, **p**eep; qua**ck**, chi**ck**, sna**ck**; goat**s**, duck**s**, kitten**s**; **ch**ew, **ch**ick).

Friday: Culminating Activity

Invite the children to bring their completed homework to circle time. Ask a volunteer to tell which number word he or she connected with the puppies. Have the volunteer hold up his or her paper and ask the class to check the answers. After all of the answers have been checked, reread the poem together one final time.

The Number Farm

One chick says "peep."
Two pigs sleep.
Three horses neigh.
Four donkeys bray.
Five puppies chew.
Six cows say "moo."
Seven goats snack.
Eight ducks say "quack."
Nine sheep have fun.
Ten kittens run.

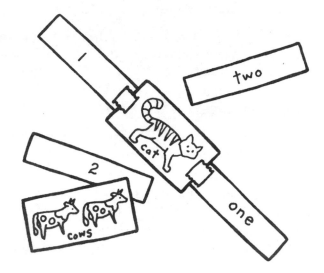

Hello,

This week we will be learning this poem about farm animals. Please read the poem with your child to help him or her learn it. Using the poem as a springboard, we will be working with singular and plural words, number words, and identifying common beginning and ending sounds in a group of words (phoneme identity) throughout the week.

Please help your child cut out the farm animals, number cards, and number word cards on the Homework Pages. Spread them out on the floor and ask your child to choose an animal card and count the animals on it. Assist your child in matching the correct number card and number word card to it. Tape the three cards together. (See the illustration above.) Continue until all the animals have been matched with the correct numbers and number words. Send the completed cards to school on _____.

Your child will be bringing home *The Number Farm* Mini Book of the poem this week. Please ask him or her to read it to you. Your child may also want to read it to a special friend or relative.

Thanks for helping us "moooove" along in our learning this year!

Sincerely,

_____

Homework Page

Directions: Cut out the animal cards and use them with the number cards on the following page.

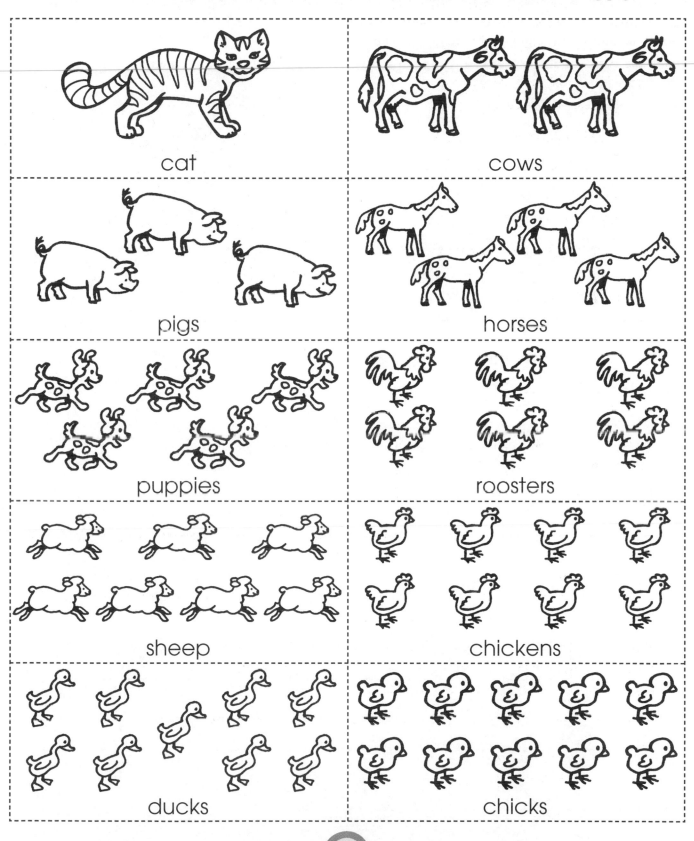

cat

cows

pigs

horses

puppies

roosters

sheep

chickens

ducks

chicks

Homework Page (cont.)

Directions: Cut out the number cards and number word cards. Spread out all the cards on the floor. Choose an animal card and count the animals on it.

Match the correct number word card and number card with each animal card. Tape the three cards together as shown on page 30.

one	two
three	four
five	six
seven	eight
nine	ten
1	2
3	4
5	6
7	8
9	10

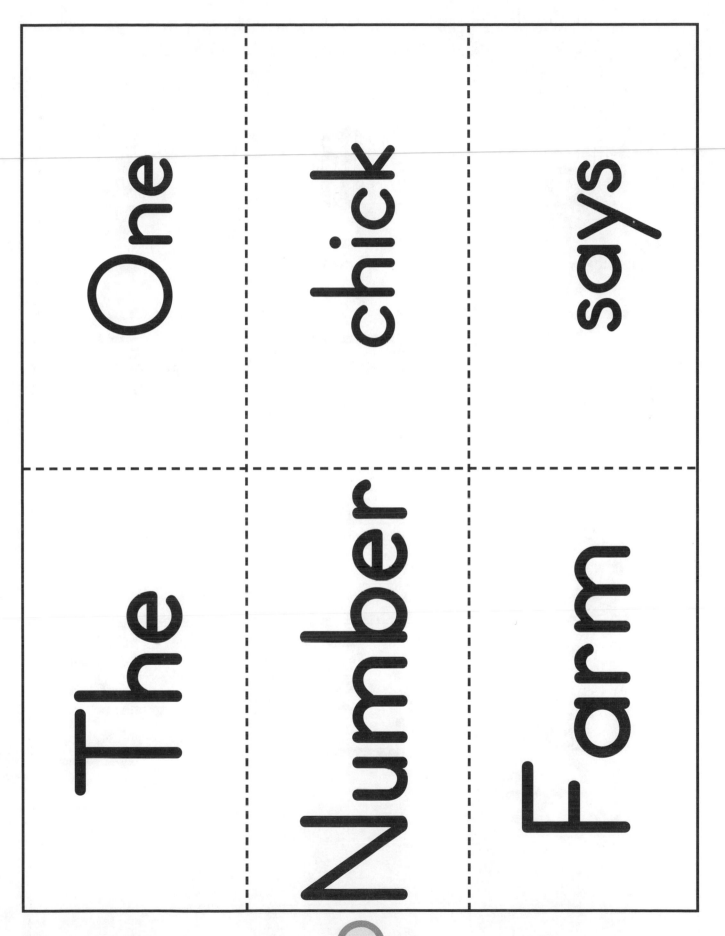

One

chick

says

The

Number

Farm

sleep.

Three

horses

"peep."

Two

pigs

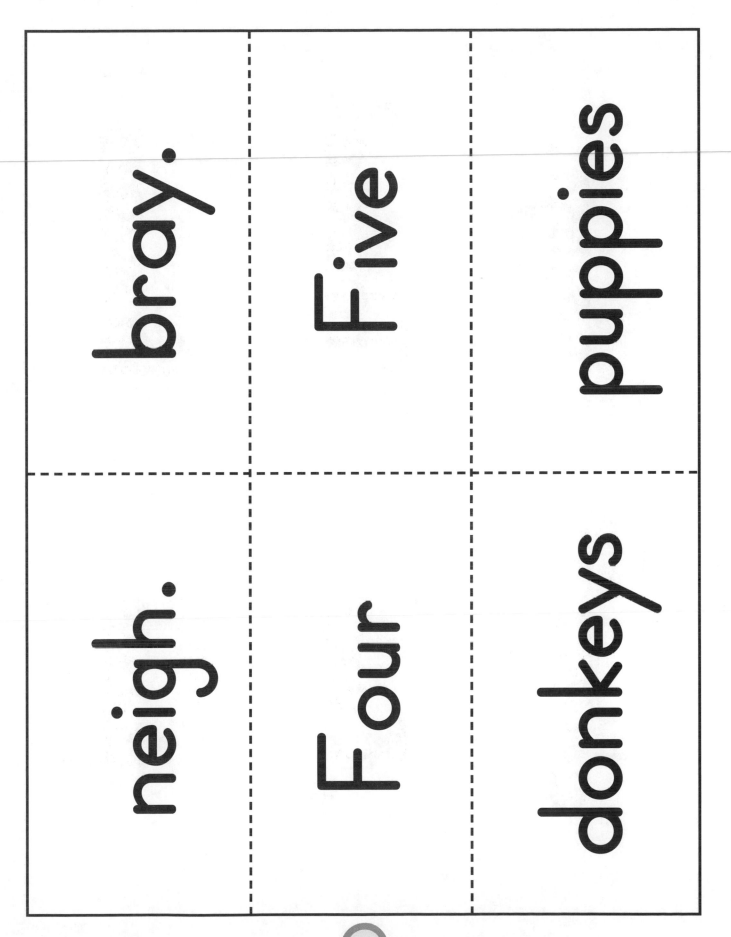

bray.

Five

puppies

neigh.

Four

donkeys

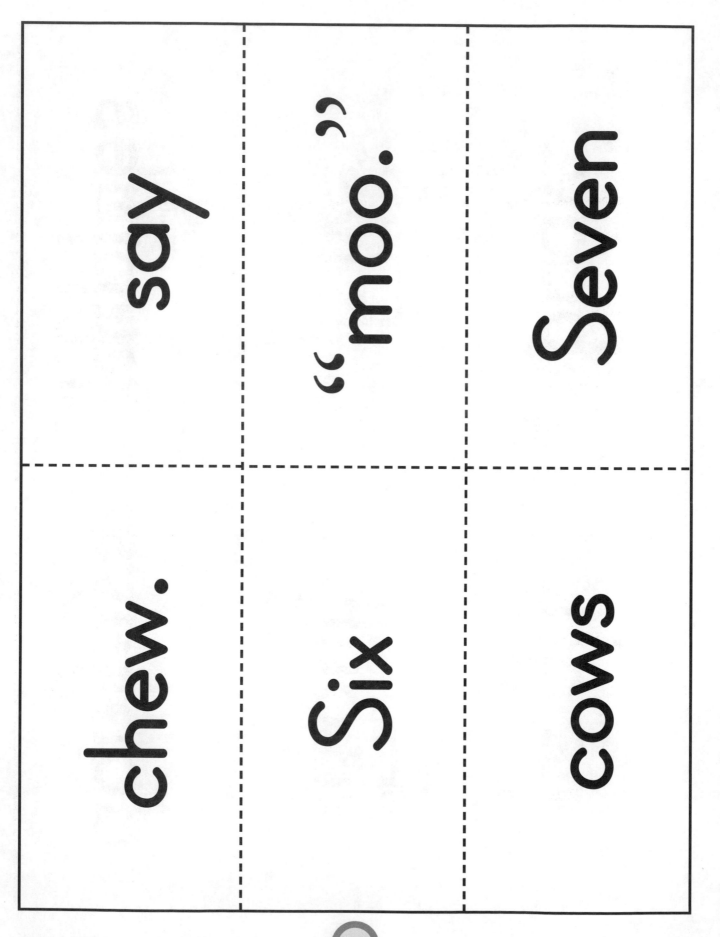

say

"moo."

Seven

chew.

Six

cows

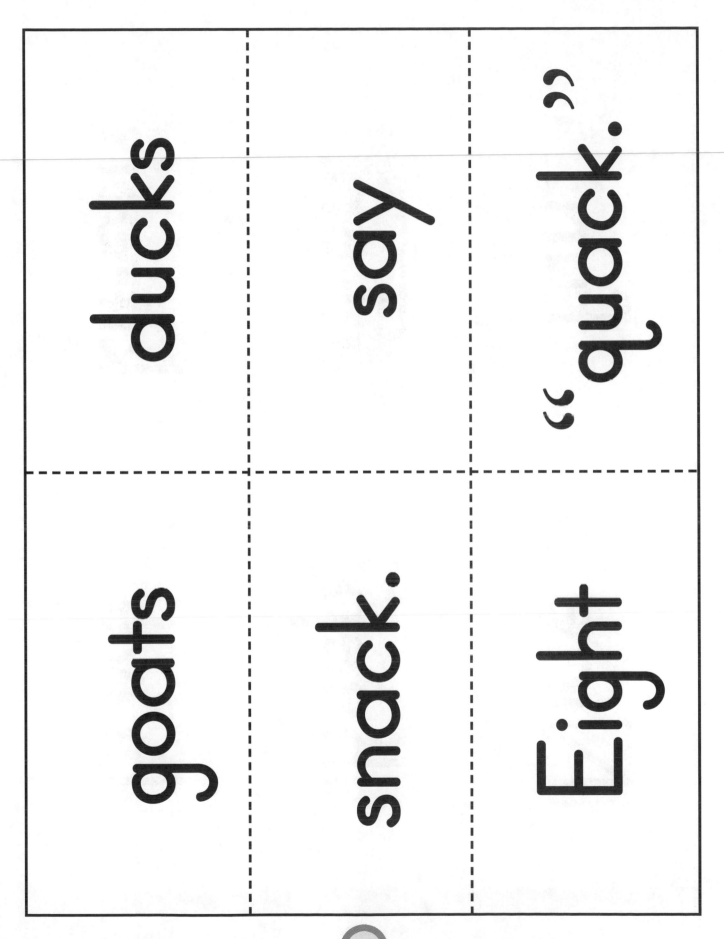

ducks

say

"quack."

goats

snack.

Eight

fun.

Ten

kittens

Nine

sheep

have

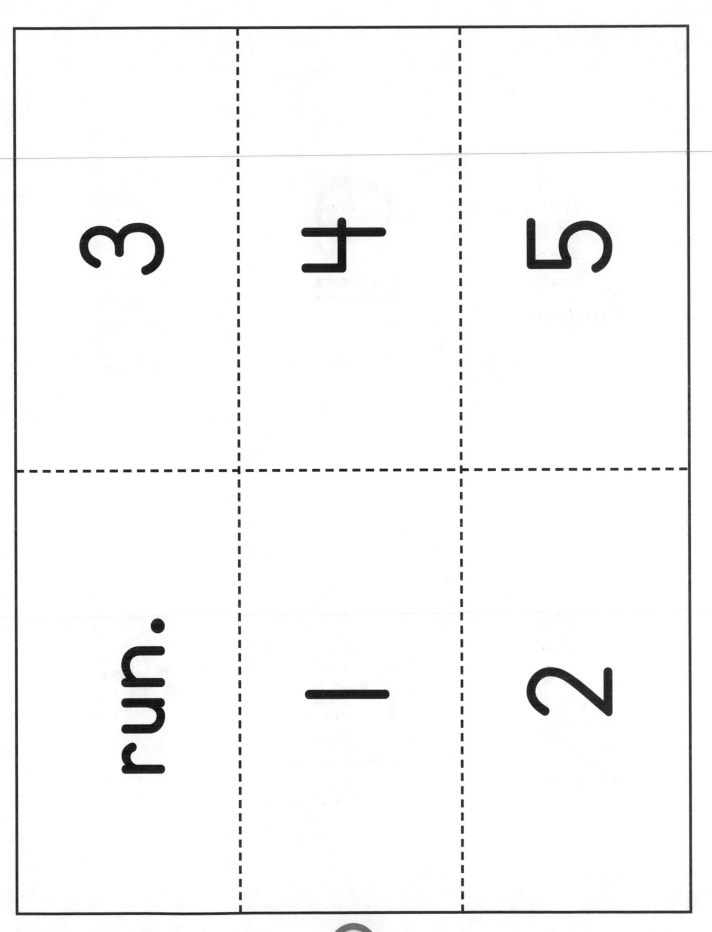

3   4   5

run.   1   2

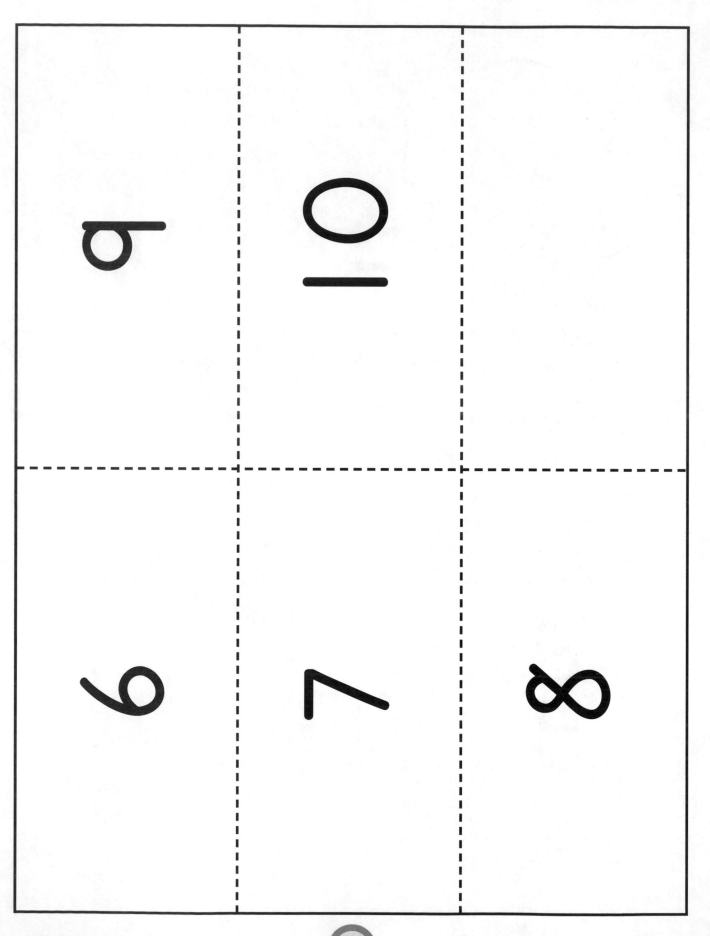

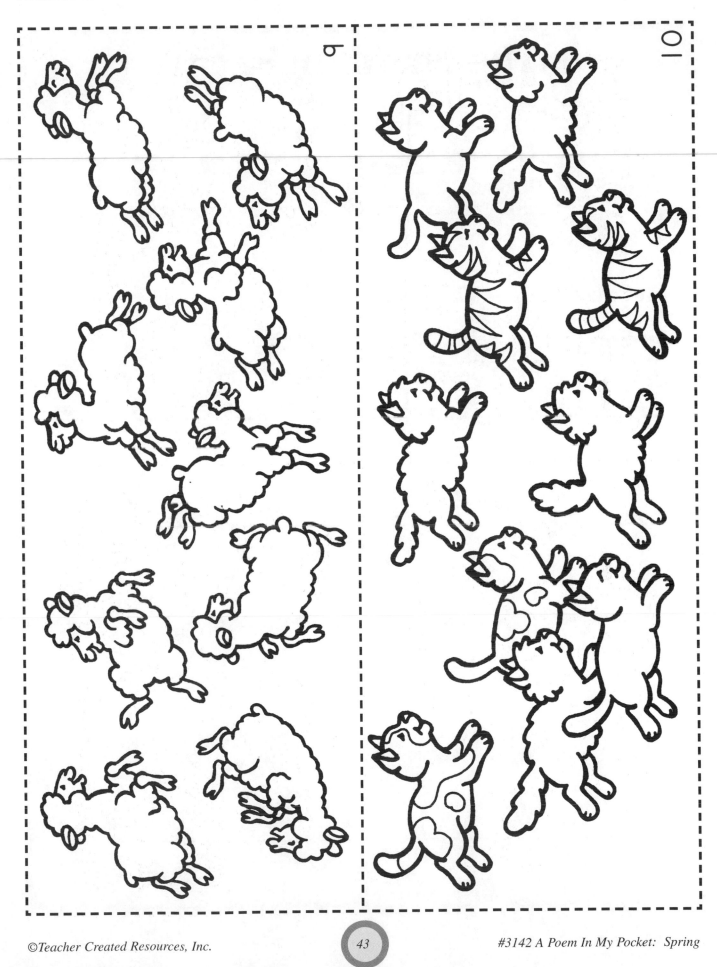

The Number Farm

One chick says "peep."

Two pigs sleep.

Three horses neigh.

Four donkeys bray.

Five puppies chew.

Six cows say "moo."

Seven goats snack.

Eight ducks say "quack."

Nine sheep have fun.

Ten kittens run.

The Number Farm

By: _____

One chick says "peep."

1

Two pigs sleep. **2**

Three horses neigh. **3**

Four donkeys bray.

④

Five puppies chew.

⑤

Six cows say "moo." **6**

Seven goats snack. **7**

Eight ducks say quack. **8**

Nine sheep have fun. **9**

Ten kittens run.

9

c a t s

Circle the "**s**" at the end of each animal name that shows there is more than one of that animal.

10

The Picnic

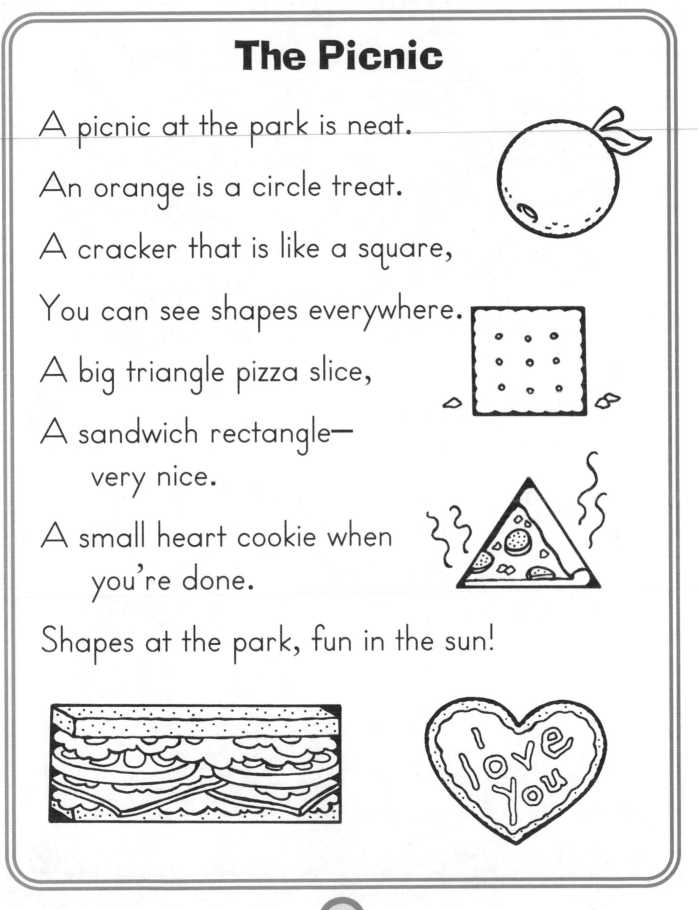

A picnic at the park is neat.

An orange is a circle treat.

A cracker that is like a square,

You can see shapes everywhere.

A big triangle pizza slice,

A sandwich rectangle—
    very nice.

A small heart cookie when
    you're done.

Shapes at the park, fun in the sun!

The Picnic

Unit Preparation

Copy and send home the Picnics Home/School Connection Parent Letter (pages 54–55). Copy and cut apart the Picnics Pocket Chart Cards (pages 56–64). Copy, color, and cut apart the Picnics Picture Cards (pages 65–66). Place all the cards in the pocket chart in the correct places. Copy, color, and cut apart the Picnics Shape Cards (page 73). Copy The Picnic Student Poem Page (page 67) and *The Picnic* Mini Book Pages (pages 68–72) for each child. See page 4 for additional preparation tips.

Student Poem Page

Talk with the children about going on a picnic. Discuss different places to take a picnic. Ask the children to think of their favorite food to eat at a picnic. Ask them what shape that food is. On the bottom of the The Picnic Student Poem Page, assist each child in writing the name of his or her favorite food on the line. Give the student time to illustrate the page with his or her favorite picnic food.

Mini Book

Assemble *The Picnic* Mini Book for each child. Have the children color the pages and read their Mini Books to others. At the end of the week, invite each child to take the book home and read it to his or her family.

Literature Links

A Picnic in October by Eve Bunting (Harcourt Children's Books, 1st edition, 1999)

The Bears' Picnic by Stan and Jan Berenstain (Random House Books for Young Readers, 1996)

The Best Picnic Ever by Clare Jarrett (Candlewick Press, 2004)

Picnic with the Pilgrims by Jane Yolen (Voyager Books, Reprint edition, 1993)

Teddy Bears' Picnic by Jimmy Kennedy (Aladdin, Reprint edition, 2000)

Pocket Chart Activities

Monday: Introduce the Poem

Read the poem, "The Picnic," aloud to the children. Reread the poem, pointing to the words as you go. Stop at each shape and ask for a volunteer to find something in the classroom that is that particular shape. If possible, bring it to the circle for everyone to see. Invite the children to read the poem aloud with you.

Tuesday: Shape Up

Read the poem together. Remove all of the cards from the pocket chart. Spread out the shape words from the poem and Picnics Shape Cards (page 73) on the floor. Ask a volunteer to come up and choose a shape and place it in the pocket chart. Ask another student to find the shape word that matches the shape and place it in the pocket chart next to the shape. Continue until all of the shapes and shape words have been matched up. Next, remove the shape cards and read the shape words together.

Wednesday: Hard and Soft C's

Explain to the class that the letter **c** makes two sounds. The first sound is /c/ as in *cat* and the second sound is /s/ as in *cereal*. Read the poem together, listening for these two sounds. Pull out the following words from the pocket chart and hand them out to seven volunteers: *picnic, cracker, can, cookie, slice, nice, circle* (this one contains both a hard and soft /c/). Read the poem, stopping at each space where a word is missing. Ask each volunteer to bring up his or her card as you come to the space where it belongs, and tell the class if his or her word contains a hard or soft /c/. Continue until all the words are replaced.

Thursday: Phoneme Addition

In Phoneme Addition, children create a new word by adding a phoneme to an existing word. For example,

> **Teacher:** What word would you have if you add /s/ to *mile*?

> **Students:** *smile.*

Use the word families *in* and *at* from the poem to practice phoneme addition by adding the following sounds to the beginning of each:

in—/b/ /f/ /p/ /s/ /t/ /w/ /sh/

at—/b/ /c/ /f/ /h/ /m/ /r/ /s/ /th/

Friday: Culminating Activity

Invite the children to bring their Homework Pages to the circle. Give each child an opportunity to share the foods he or she drew for each shape. Keep a tally of the foods that were used by more than one student to see what the most popular choice was for each shape. Reread the poem one more time to wrap up the unit.

The Picnic

A picnic at the park is neat.
An orange is a circle treat.
A cracker that is like a square,
You can see shapes everywhere.
A big triangle pizza slice,
A sandwich rectangle—very nice.
A small heart cookie when you're done.
Shapes at the park, fun in the sun!

Hello,

This week we will be learning this poem about picnics. Please read the poem with your child to help him or her learn it. Using the poem as a springboard, we will be working with shapes and shape words, hard and soft /c/ (hard /c/ as in *cracker*, soft c as in *nice*), as well as adding sounds to a word to form a new word (phoneme addition) throughout the week. (For example, add /b/ to the beginning of *at* to get *bat*.)

Please help your child pack a picnic of shape foods using the Homework Page. Ask your child to think of foods he or she would like to take on a picnic. Encourage your child to think of foods that are different from the ones in the poem. After he or she has picked a food, help your child identify what shape it is. Using a crayon or markers, have your child draw the food inside the shape provided and assist him or her in writing the name of the food on the line below it. Continue until all of the shapes have been completed.

Please send the completed homework to school on _____.

Your child will be bringing home *The Picnic* Mini Book this week. Please ask him or her to read it to you. He or she may also want to read it to a special friend or relative.

Learning is a "picnic" for your child when you are involved!

Sincerely,

_____

Homework Page

Directions: Have your child think of picnic foods that are different from the ones in the poem. After picking a food, your child should identify what shape it is.

Using a crayon or markers, have your child draw the food on the shape provided. Help him or her write the name of the food on the line below it. Continue until all of the shapes have been completed.

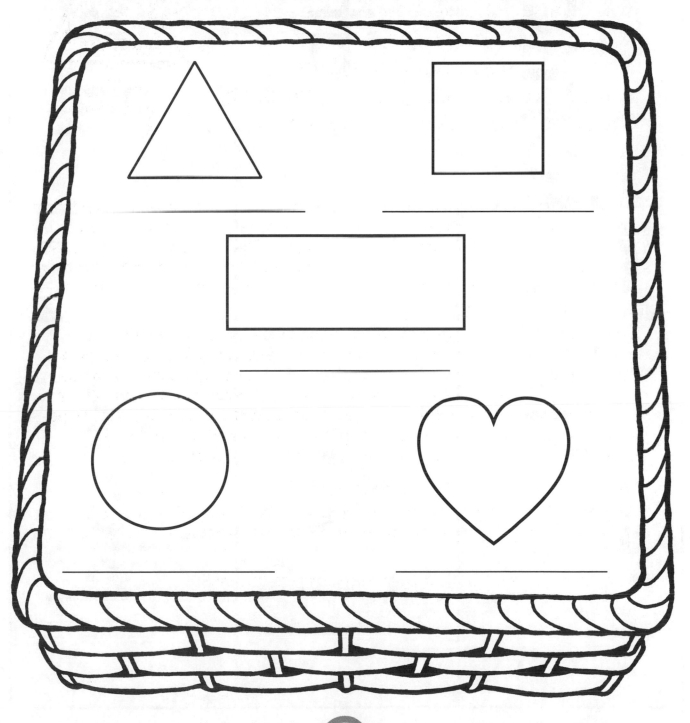

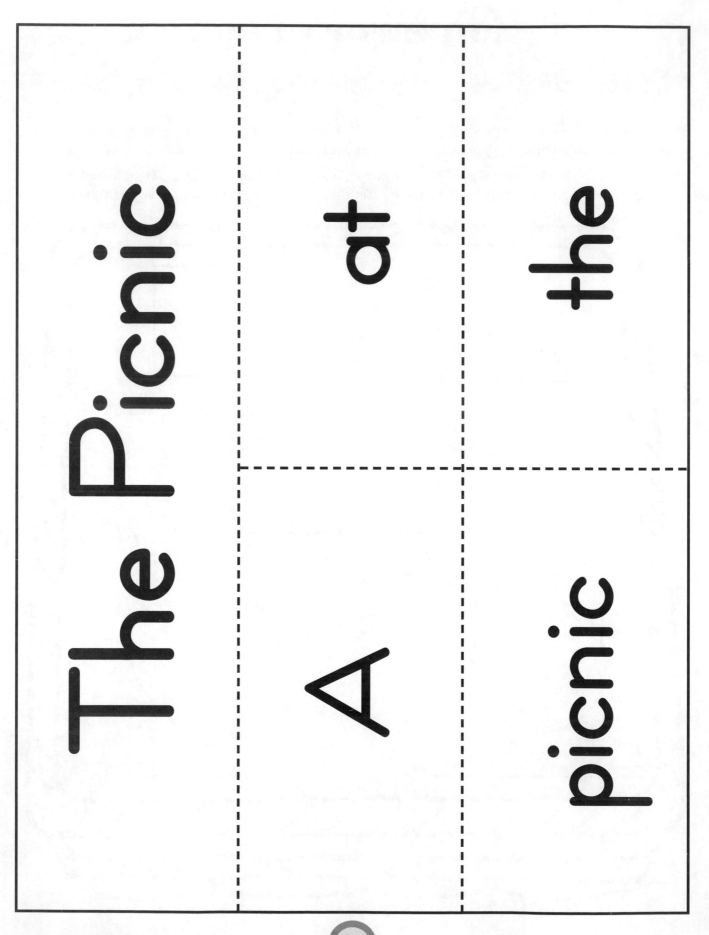

The Picnic

at

the

A

picnic

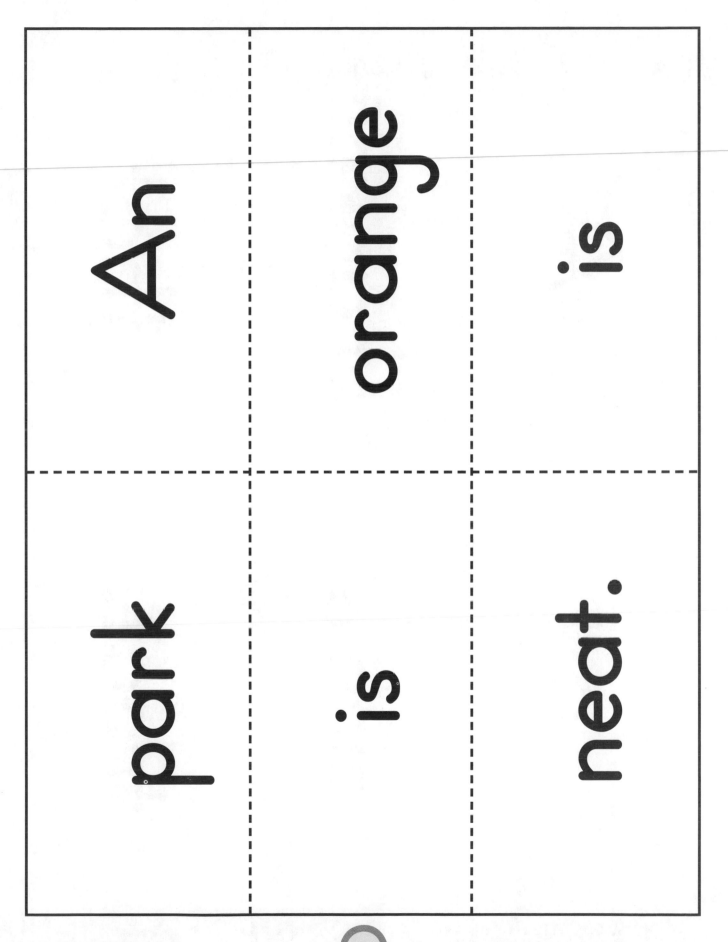

An

orange

is

park

is

neat.

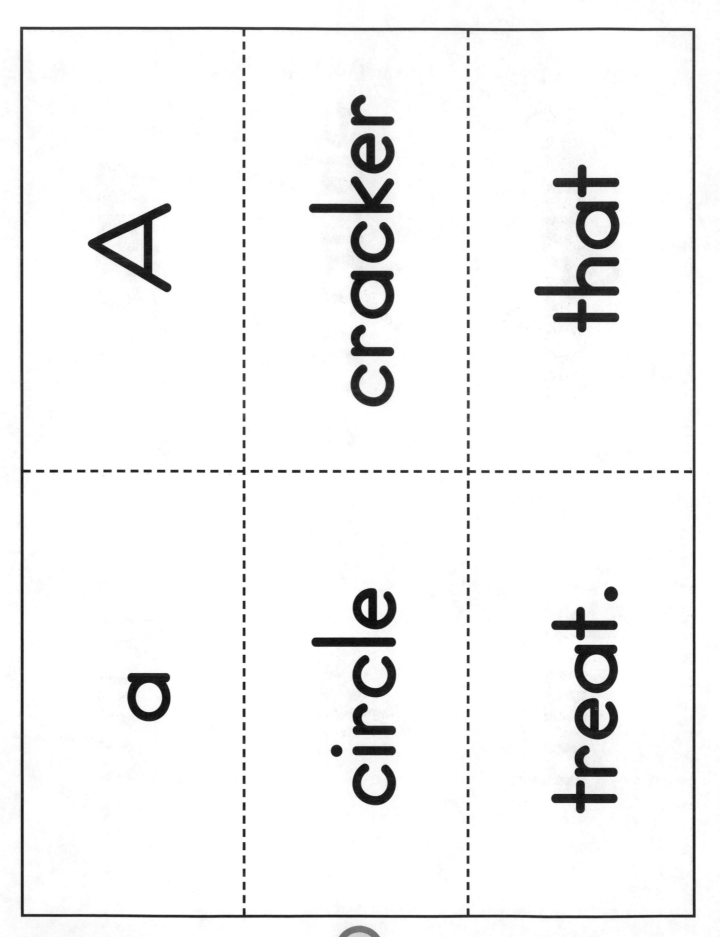

A

cracker

that

a

circle

treat.

square,

You

can

is

like

a

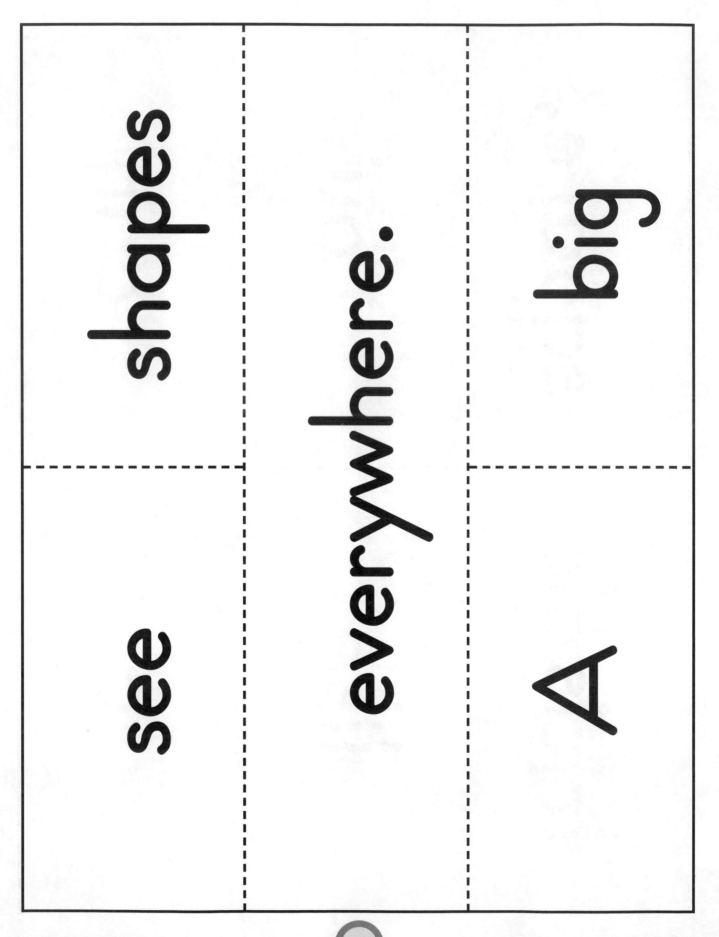

shapes

see

everywhere.

big

A

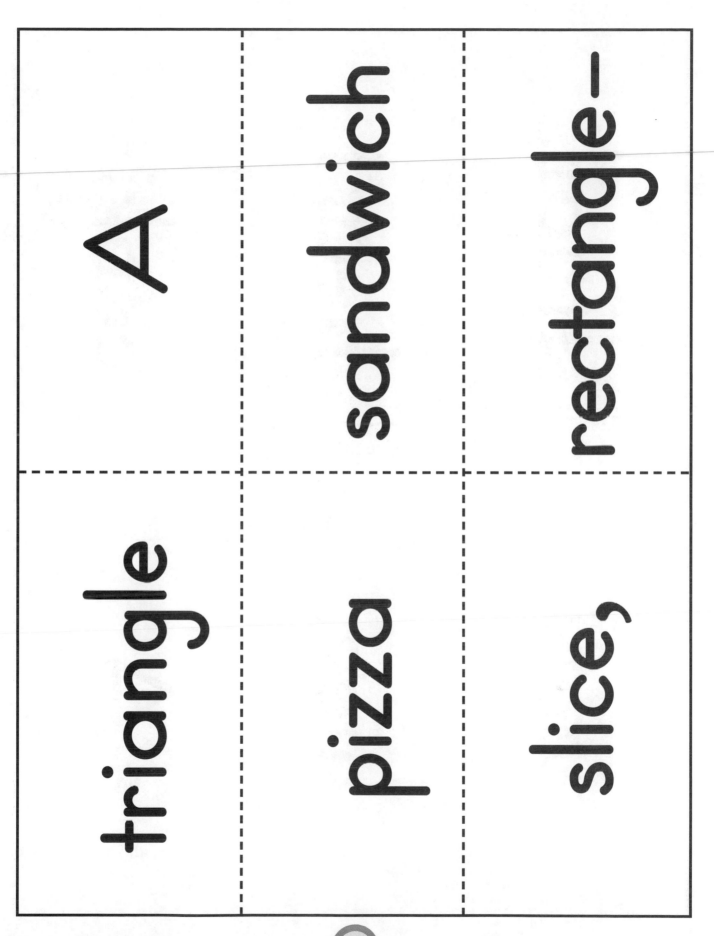

A

sandwich

rectangle—

triangle

pizza

slice,

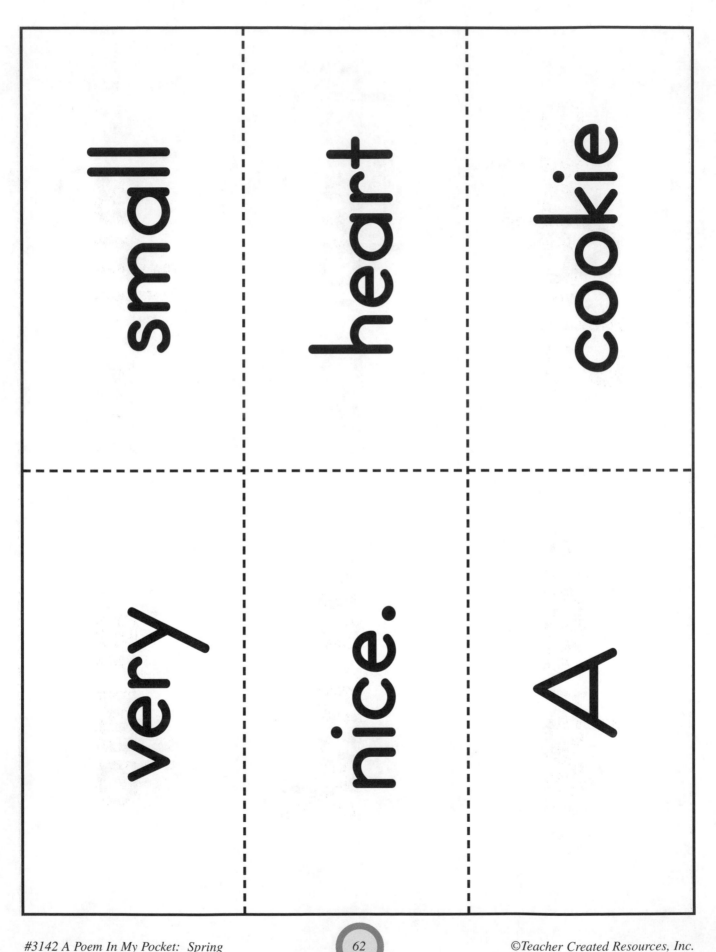

small

heart

cookie

very

nice.

A

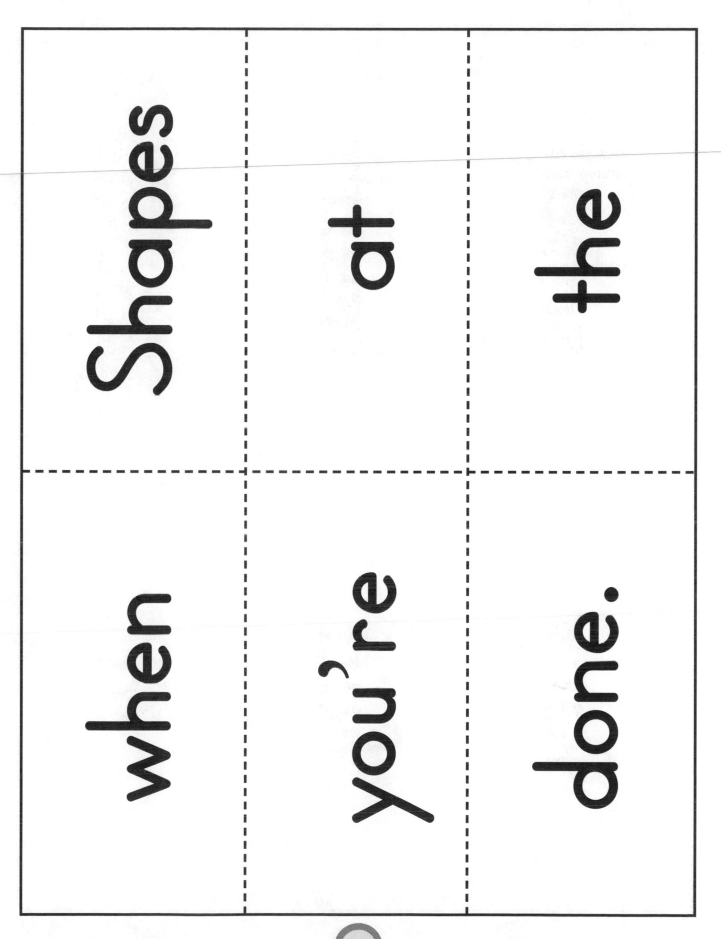

Shapes

at

the

when

you're

done.

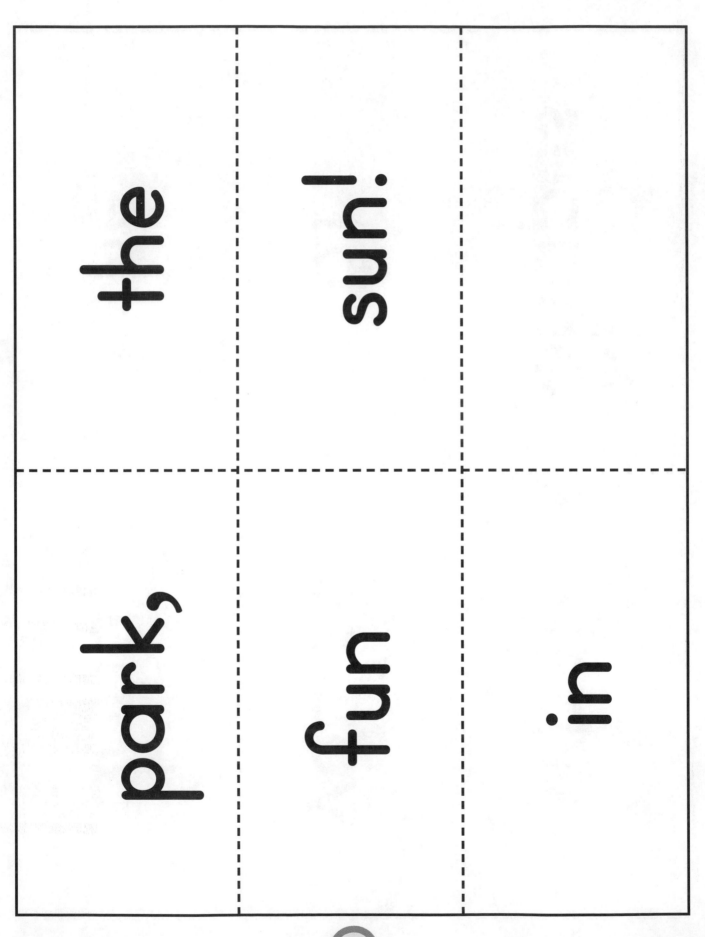

the

sun!

park,

fun

in

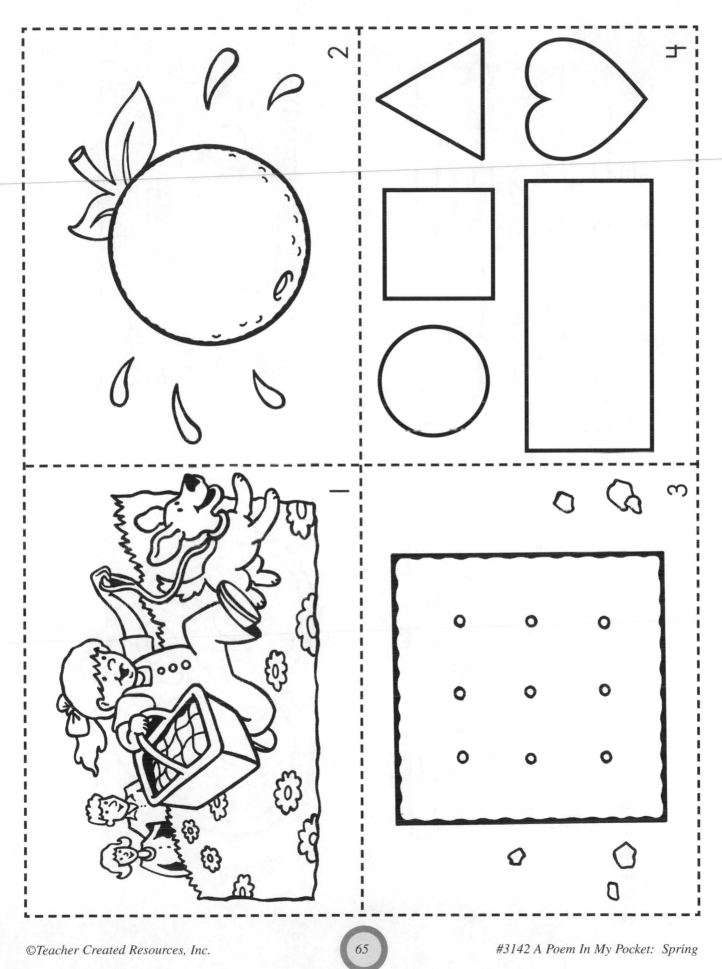

        #3142 A Poem In My Pocket: Spring

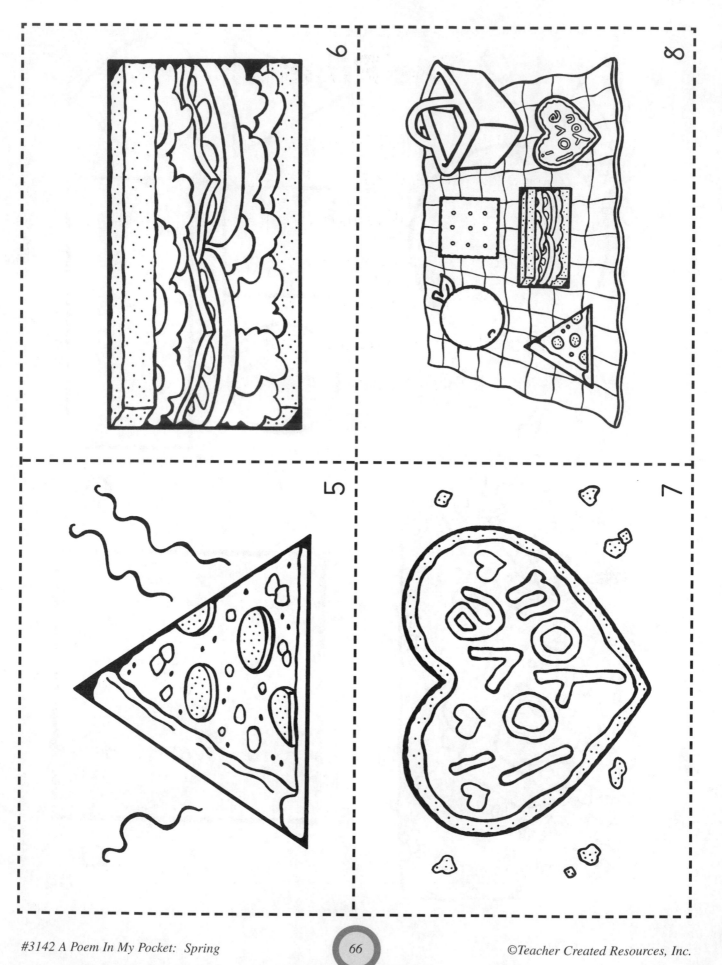

The Picnic

A picnic at the park is neat.

An orange is a circle treat.

A cracker that is like a square,

You can see shapes everywhere.

A big triangle pizza slice,

A sandwich rectangle—very nice.

A small heart cookie when you're done.

Shapes at the park, fun in the sun!

I like to eat _____ at a picnic.

The Picnic

By: _____

A picnic at the park is neat.

1

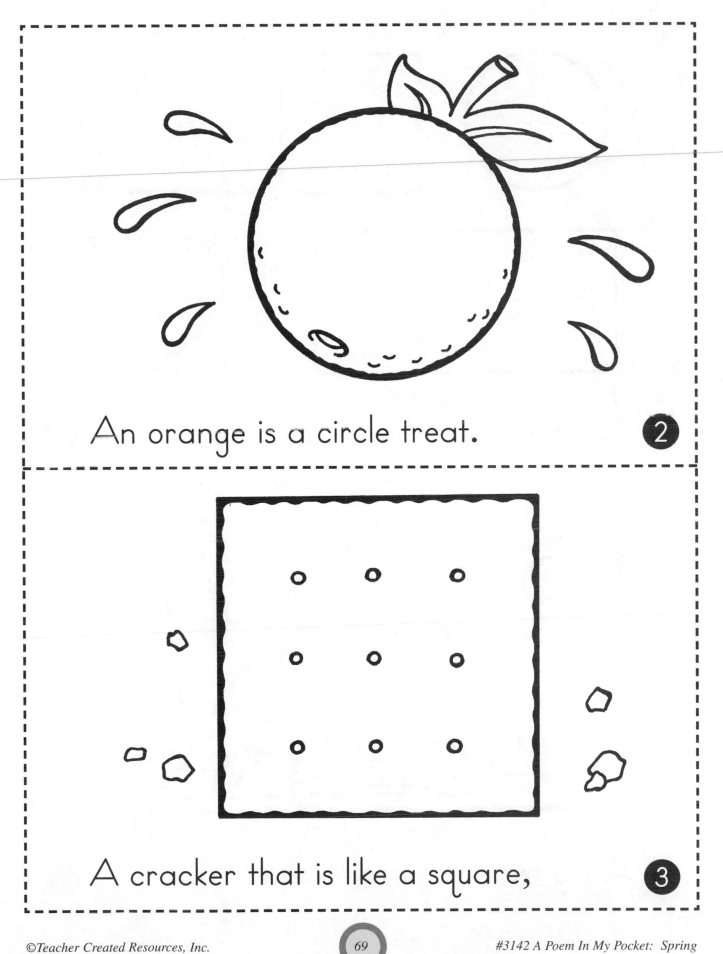

An orange is a circle treat.

2

A cracker that is like a square,

3

You can see shapes everywhere. **4**

A big triangle pizza slice, **5**

A sandwich rectangle—very nice.   **6**

A small heart cookie when you're done.   **7**

Shapes at the park, fun in the sun!   **8**

circle

Circle the word that contains a **c** that makes the /s/ sound.   **9**

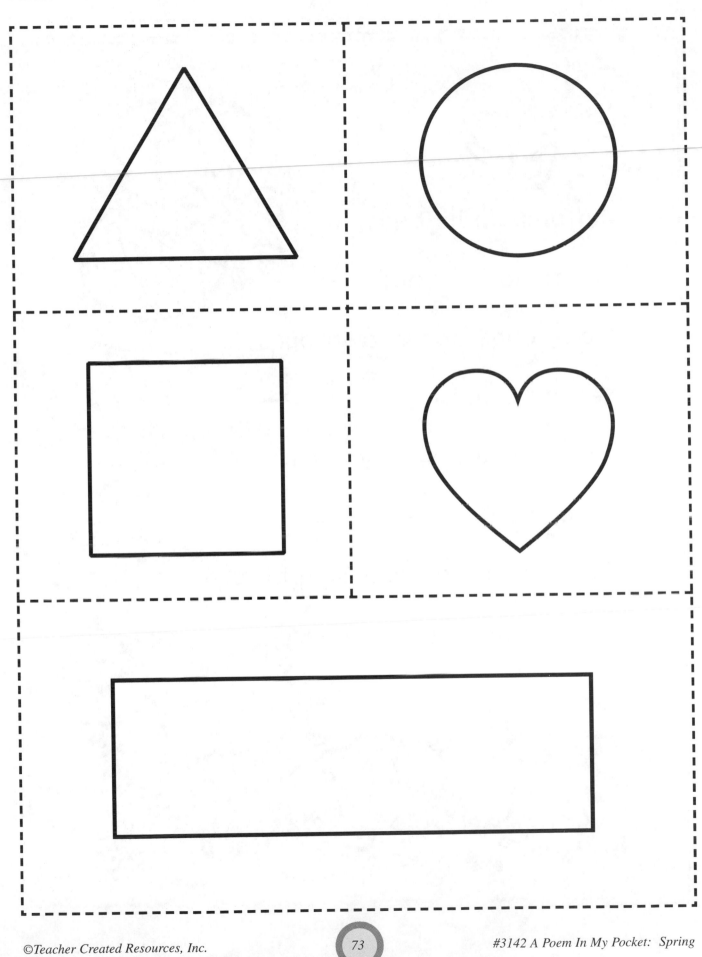

#3142 A Poem In My Pocket: Spring

Bugs

Big bugs, little bugs,

What do they do?

Black bugs and brown bugs,

Red bugs too.

Fat bugs and skinny bugs,

Creeping on your shoe.

Flying bugs and crawling bugs,

Coming after you!

Bugs

Unit Preparation

Copy and send home the Bugs Home/School Connection Parent Letter (pages 77–79). Copy and cut apart the Bugs Pocket Chart Cards (pages 80–85). (**Note:** You will need to cut the periods, question mark, and exclamation mark off of the cards for Thursday's activity.) Copy, appropriately color, and cut out the Bugs Picture Cards (pages 86–87). Place all the cards in the pocket chart in the correct places. Copy the Bugs Student Poem Page (page 88) and the *Bugs* Mini Book pages (pages 89–93) for each child. Copy, appropriately color, and cut out (as indicated) the Bug Cards (page 94). See page 4 for additional preparation tips.

Student Poem Page

Ask children to list bugs they have seen. Talk about the different characteristics of bugs (e.g., size, color, and shape). Ask each child to think about two words that could describe a bug (for example, *big* and *black*). Assist the child in writing the words on the two blanks at the bottom of the Bugs Student Poem Page. Have each child draw his or her bug in the space provided.

Mini Book

Assemble a *Bugs* Mini Book for each child. Have the children color the pages using the appropriate colors and read the Mini Books to others. At the end of the week, invite each child to take the book home and read it to his or her family.

Literature Links

Bugs! by David T. Greenberg (Megan Tingley, 1st edition, 1997)

How Many Bugs in a Box? by David A. Carter (Little Simon, 1988)

The Icky Bug Alphabet Book by Jeremy Pallotta (Charlesbridge Publishing, 1978)

I Like Bugs by Margaret Wise Brown (Random House Books for Young Readers, 1999)

Snappy Little Bugs by Clare Nielson (Millbrook Press, Pop-up edition, 1999)

Pocket Chart Activities

Monday: Introduce the Poem

Ask students to name bugs that they like and bugs that they don't like. Read the poem, "Bugs," aloud to the children. Reread the poem, pointing to the words as you go. Invite the children to read the poem with you.

Tuesday: Search and Sort

Invite the children to help you recite the poem aloud, pointing to the words as you go. Remove all of the words from the pocket chart except for the following: *big, little, red, brown,* and *black*. Put the words *big* and *little* on opposite sides of the top line of the pocket chart and read them with the class. Spread out the Bug Cards (page 94) on the floor. Have each child take a turn finding a bug card and placing it on the correct side of the chart according to its size. Next, draw a chart on the board or chart paper. Remove the Bug Cards and words from the pocket chart. Use the Pocket Chart Cards (*big, little, red, brown,* and *black*) to label the chart as indicated. Explain that you are now going to sort the bugs by looking at more than one characteristic. Demonstrate how to put the bugs on the chart by picking up a bug, first deciding if it is big or little to determine which row it will go in, and then putting it in the proper column according to its color. After the children have helped you place all the bugs on the chart, look at the bugs in each box and notice that they all have the same two characteristics (for example, all of these bugs are big and red).

	red	brown	black
big			
little			

Wednesday: Phoneme Segmentation

In Phoneme Segmentation, children break a word into separate sounds. For example,

Teacher: How many sounds are in *chip*? **Students:** /ch/ /i/ /p/. There are three sounds in *chip*.

Use the following words from the poem to practice phoneme segmentation as indicated above: *bugs, red, big,* and *fat*.

Thursday: Playing with Punctuation

Read the poem with your class. Reread the poem, stopping each time you come to a punctuation mark. Talk about what job each punctuation mark does. Remove a period, question mark, and exclamation mark. Rearrange them in the poem and read each line with its new punctuation. Repeat this activity several times until the children are familiar with what each punctuation mark does.

Friday: Culminating Activity

Invite the children to bring their Homework Pages to the circle and hold them up for the class to see. Ask the children to switch papers with a friend. Have the children look at the bugs in each box together to be sure they were put in the correct places on the chart. Allow the children to make any necessary corrections to their papers, then read the poem together one final time.

Bugs

Big bugs, little bugs,
What do they do?
Black bugs and brown bugs,
Red bugs too.
Fat bugs and skinny bugs,
Creeping on your shoe.
Flying bugs and crawling bugs,
Coming after you!

Hello,

This week we will be learning this poem about bugs. Please read the poem with your child to help him or her learn it. Using the poem as a springboard, we will be working with sorting and classifying, punctuation, and breaking words into separate sounds (phoneme segmentation).

Please assist your child in cutting out the bug cards on the Homework Page. Spread out the cards on a table or the floor and look at each to determine which bug is fat or skinny, flying or crawling. Turn the chart so that the words *crawling* & *flying* are on top. Place each card in the correct box on the attached Homework Chart according to the characteristics listed. When the bugs are sorted, attach them to the Homework Chart with glue or tape. Please send the completed homework to school on _____.

Your child will be bringing home a *Bugs* Mini Book this week. Please ask him or her to read it to you. He or she may also want to read it to a special friend or relative.

Thanks for helping us "buzzzzz" along!

Sincerely,

_____

Homework Page

Directions: Cut out the bug cards and use them with the chart on page 79.

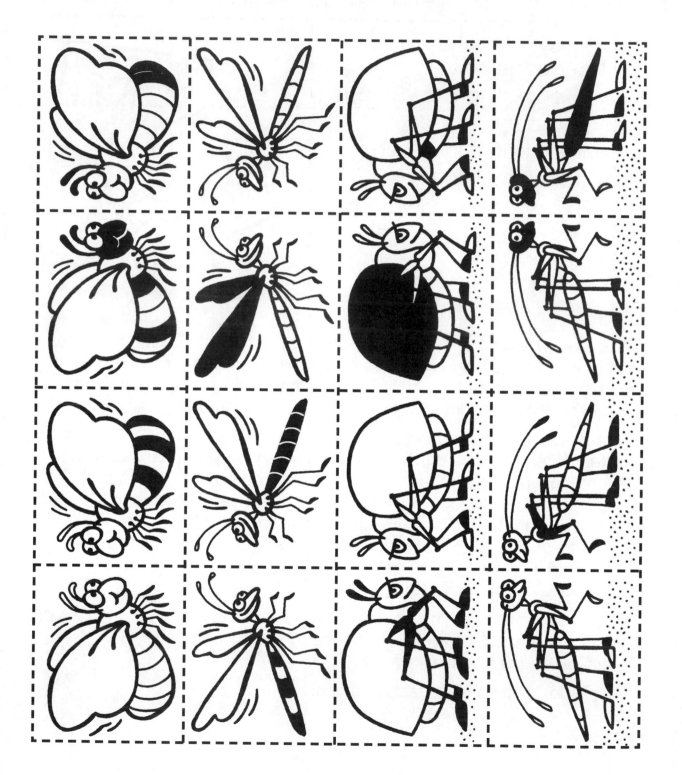

Homework Chart

Directions: Spread out the bug cards on a table or the floor. Look at each card to determine which is fat or skinny, flying or crawling. Using glue or tape, attach each card to the correct box on the chart.

	fat	skinny
flying		
crawling		

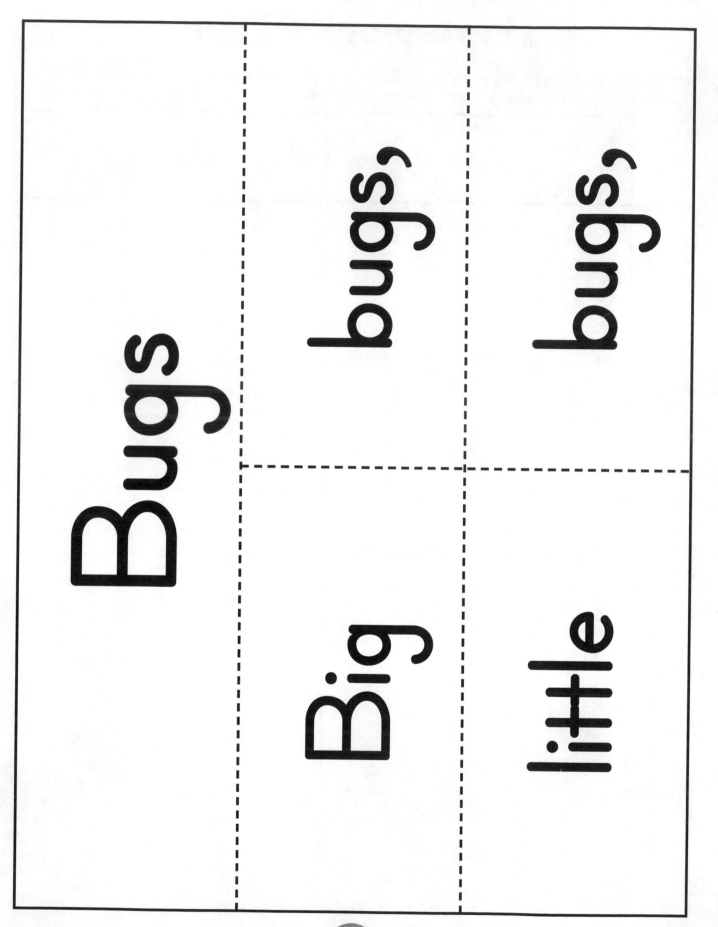

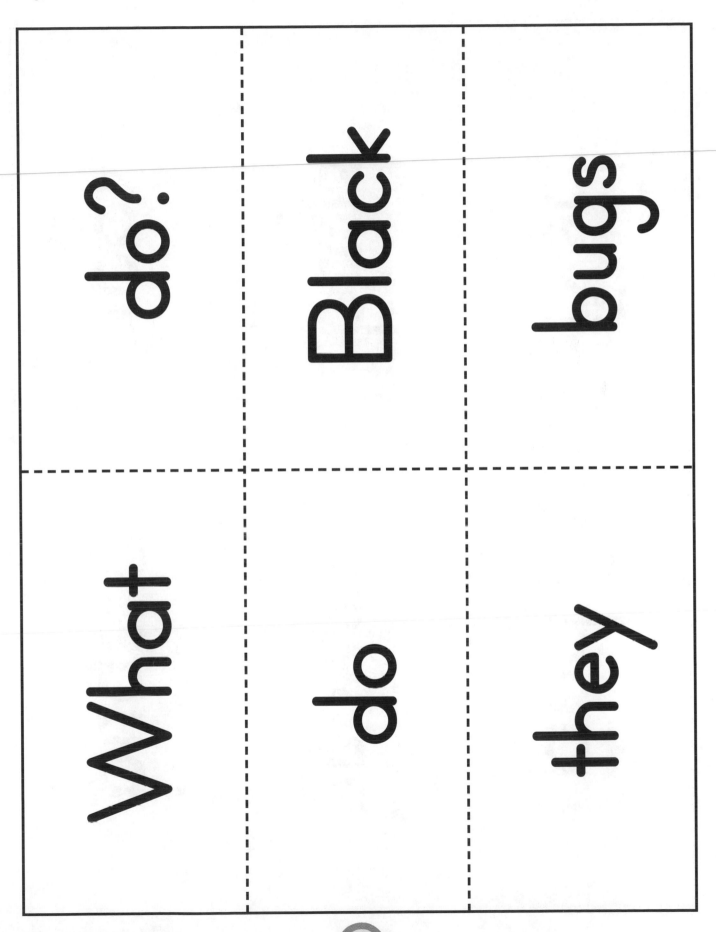

do?

Black

bugs

What

do

they

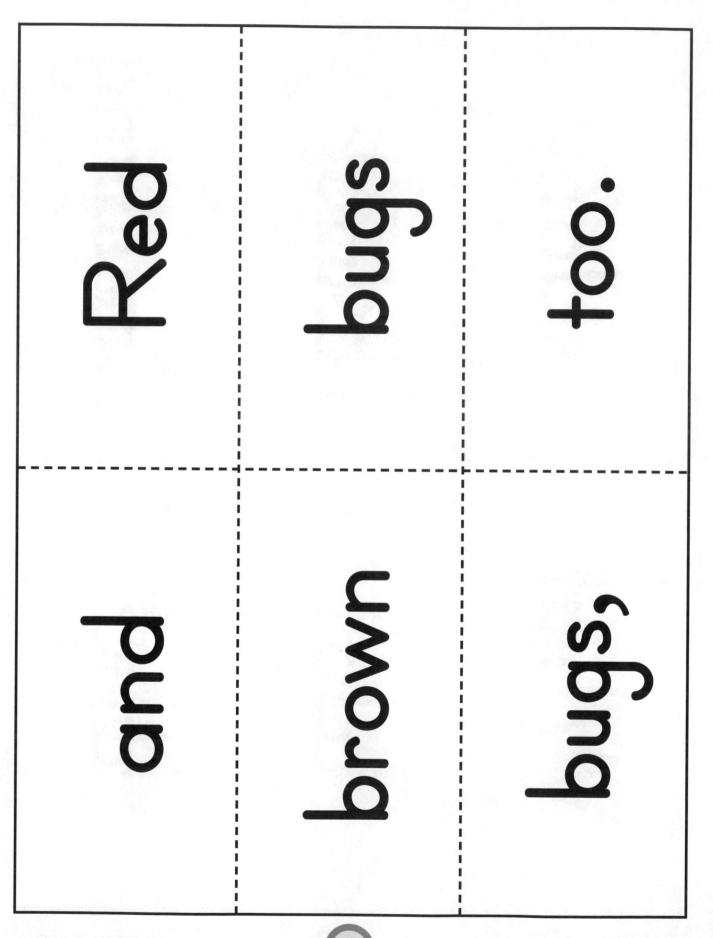

Red bugs too.

and brown bugs,

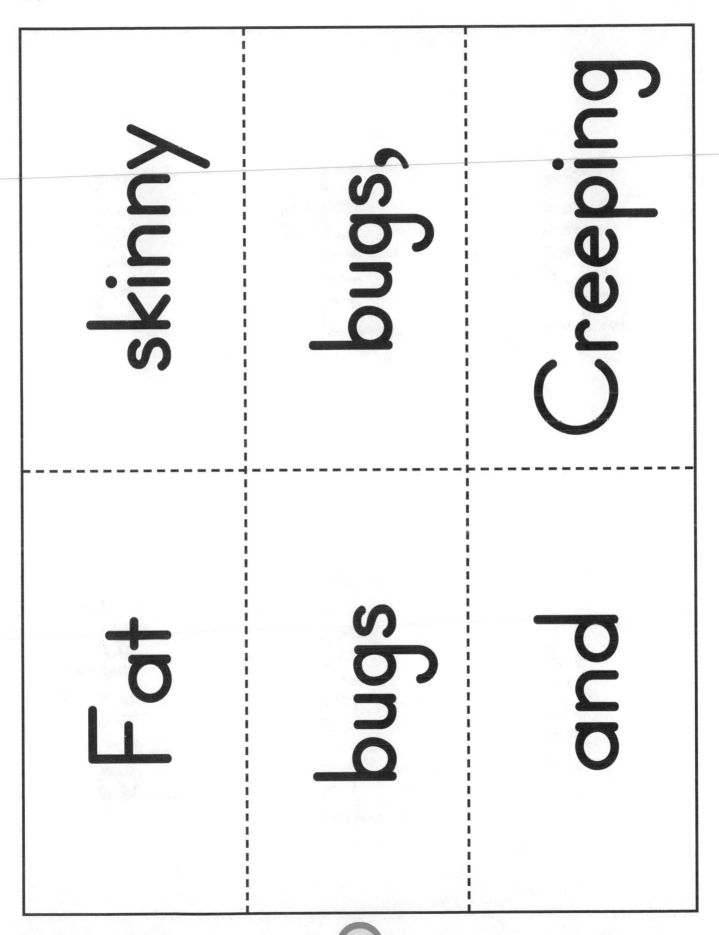

skinny

bugs,

Creeping

Fat

bugs

and

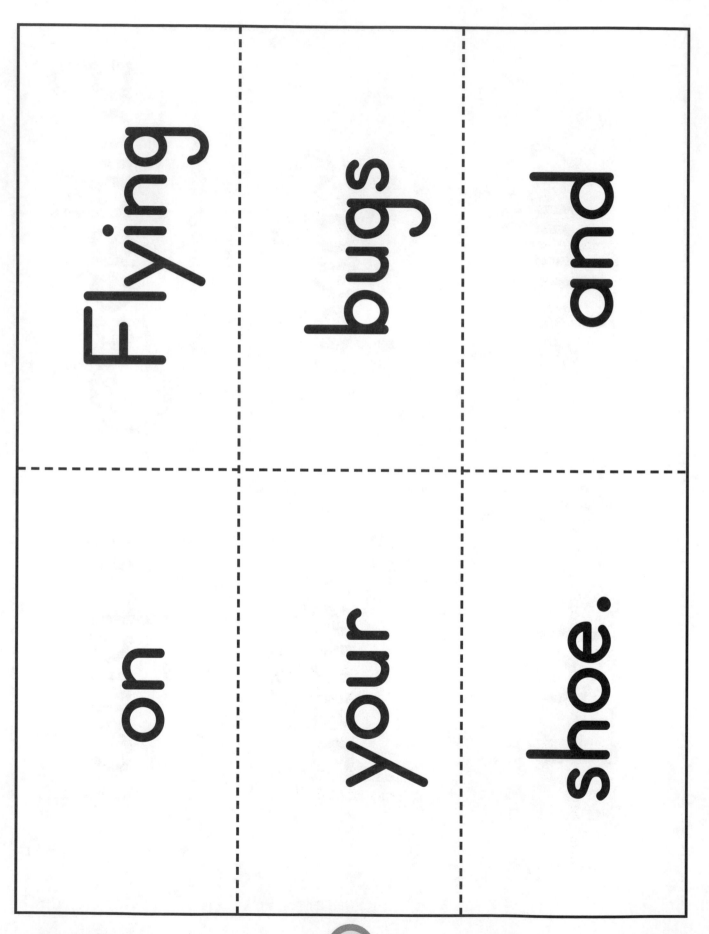

Flying

bugs

and

on

your

shoe.

84

after

you!

crawling

bugs,

Coming

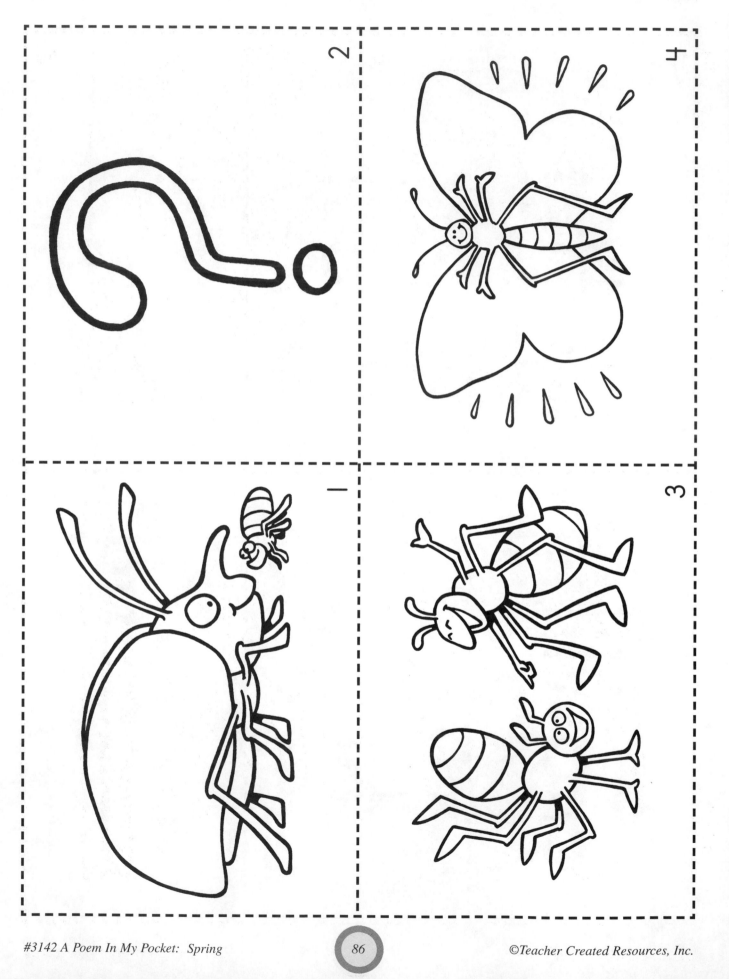

Bugs

Big bugs, little bugs,
What do they do?
Black bugs and brown bugs,
Red bugs too.
Fat bugs and skinny bugs,
Creeping on your shoe.
Flying bugs and crawling bugs,
Coming after you!

My _____, _____ bug.

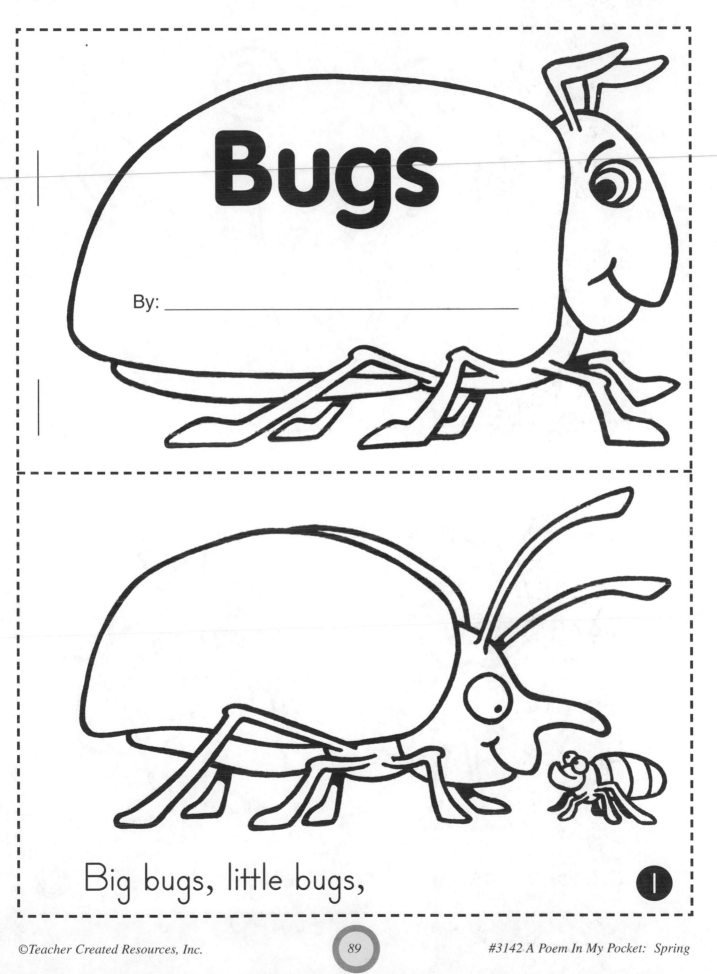

Bugs

By: _____

Big bugs, little bugs,

1

What do they do?

2

Black bugs and brown bugs,

3

Red bugs too.　④

Fat bugs and skinny bugs,　⑤

#3142 A Poem In My Pocket: Spring

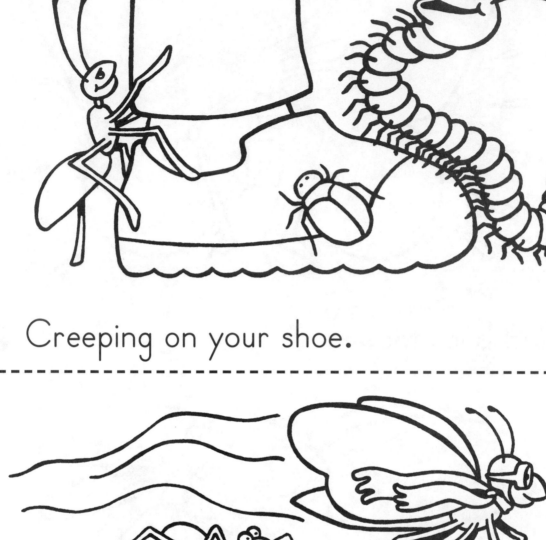

Creeping on your shoe.   6

Flying bugs and crawling bugs,   7

Coming after you!

8

Circle all of the punctuation marks in the book.

9

Teacher Directions: Color the bugs in the first row red. Color the bugs in the second row brown. Color the bugs in the third row black. Cut out the cards and laminate.

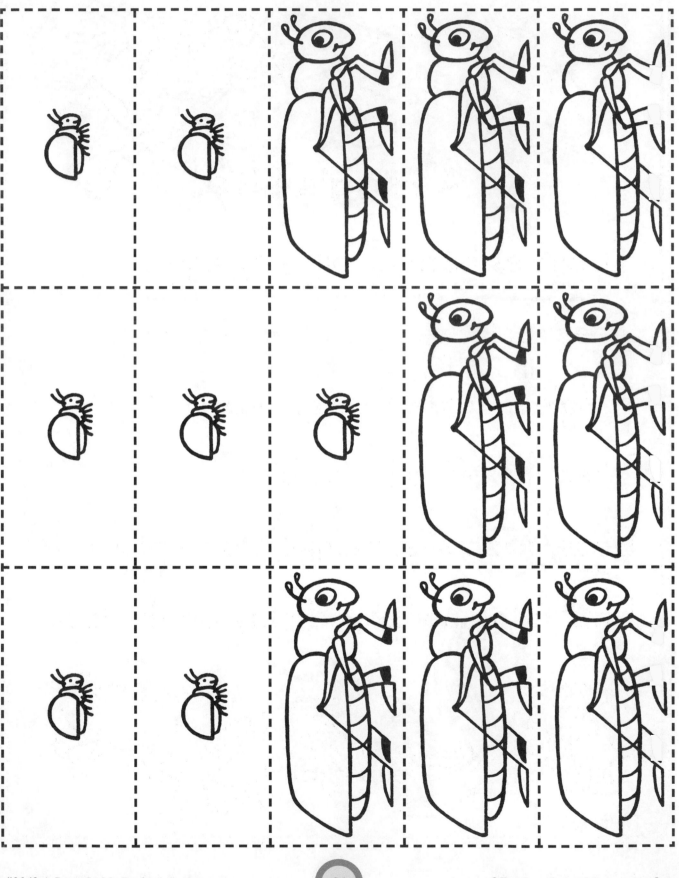

A Frog's Life

Tadpoles hatch from tiny eggs.

The froglet grows a tail and legs.

Froglet's tail will disappear.

Then it's a frog, it is clear!

Eggs, tadpoles, froglets, and frogs

Live in the pond and play on the logs.

Frogs

Unit Preparation

Copy and send home the Frogs Home/School Connection Parent Letter (page 98). Copy and cut apart the Frogs Pocket Chart Cards and Picture Cards (pages 99–107). Appropriately color the picture cards. Place all the cards in the pocket chart in the correct places. Copy the Frogs Student Poem Page (page 108) and *A Frog's Life* Mini Book (pages 109–112) for each child. See page 4 for additional preparation tips.

Poem Page

Present each child with a copy of A Frog's Life (page 95) after they have become familiar with the poem. Discuss the illustrations, naming each stage of the frog's life. Compare each stage. Discuss how tiny the frog eggs are. Describe the shape of the tadpole. Mention that tadpoles grow two back legs and then two front legs. Count the froglet's four legs. How is a frog different from a tadpole?

Ask the children to decide which stage of the frog's life cycle is their favorite—egg, tadpole, froglet, or frog. Give children a copy of the Frogs Student Poem Page (page 108). Guide them in writing the word on the blank line on the Poem Page, or write it for them. Allow time to make and color the illustrations.

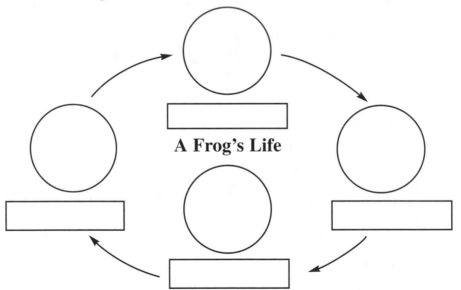

A Frog's Life

Mini Book

Assemble a *A Frog's Life* Mini Book for each child. Have the children color the pages and read their books to others. At the end of the week, invite each child to take the book home and read it to his or her family.

Literature Links

Frog and Toad Together by Arnold Lobel (Scholastic, 1999)

Frogs by Gail Gibbons (Holiday House, 1994)

From Tadpole to Frog by Wendy Pfeffer (HarperTrophy, 1994)

The Icky Sticky Frog by Dawn Bentley and Salina Yoon (Piggy Toes Press, 1999)

Jump, Frog, Jump by Robert Kalan (Greenwillow, 1995)

Pocket Chart Activities

Monday: Introduce the Poem

Ask the children which pet they would choose if they could have an egg, tadpole, froglet, or frog. Ask them to explain their choice. Read the poem, "A Frog's Life," aloud to the children. Reread the poem, pointing to the words as you go. Invite the children to read the poem aloud with you.

Tuesday: Circle of Life

After the children are familiar with the poem, draw the diagram (page 96) on the board or chart paper. Explain to the children that a frog's life is like a circle because it continues to go on as frogs lay eggs and start the cycle again. Tell the children that the first circle represents the egg stage of a frog's life. Have two students come up and find the corresponding picture card and word card and attach them to the chart in the correct place. Continue in this manner with each stage of the frog's life until the chart is complete. Review the life cycle of the frog again to be sure all of your students are familiar with it.

Wednesday: Phoneme Substitution

In phoneme substitution, children are able to remove one sound from a word and replace it with other sounds to create new words. Point to each word in the poem and read it aloud. Next, ask the children to replace the first sound with a different sound. For example: *hatch*, replace the /h/ with /m/. What is the new word? (*match*)

hatch: replace the /h/ with /m/, /c/, /p/

logs: replace the /l/ with /d/, /h/, /j/

tail: replace the /t/ with /r/, /n/, /s/

Thursday: Fill in the Blank

Remove the words *eggs*, *tadpoles*, *froglet*, and *frog* from the pocket chart and spread them out on the floor so the children can see them. Have the children help you read the poem, pausing where each missing word card belongs. Have the children help you determine which word goes in each blank. Find the missing word card and place it in the correct place on the chart.

Friday: Culminating Activity

Ask the children to bring their completed homework A Frog's Life Poem Pages to the circle. Review the Frog Lifecycle and have the children share their own life cycle pictures with the class. Review the poem and life cycle of a frog with your students for a final time.

A Frog's Life

Tadpoles hatch from tiny eggs.
The froglet grows a tail and legs.
Froglet's tail will disappear.
Then it's a frog, it is clear!
Eggs, tadpoles, froglets, and frogs
Live in the pond and play on the logs.

Hello,

This week we will be learning this poem about a frog's life cycle. Using the poem as a springboard, we will be working on life cycles, sequencing, and changing sounds in words to create new words (phoneme substitution) throughout the week. Please read the poem with your child to help him or her learn it.

Please help your child find or draw three pictures of himself or herself at different ages to represent the life cycle to this point. For example, you may include a baby picture, a toddler picture, and a current picture. Arrange the pictures in order and tape them on a separate piece of paper, writing the numbers 1, 2, and 3 under each to indicate the correct order. Please send the completed page to school with your child on

_____.

Your child will be bringing home *A Frog's Life* Mini Book of the poem this week. Please ask him or her to read it to you. Your child may also want to read it to a special friend or relative.

Thank you for your participation!

Sincerely,

_____

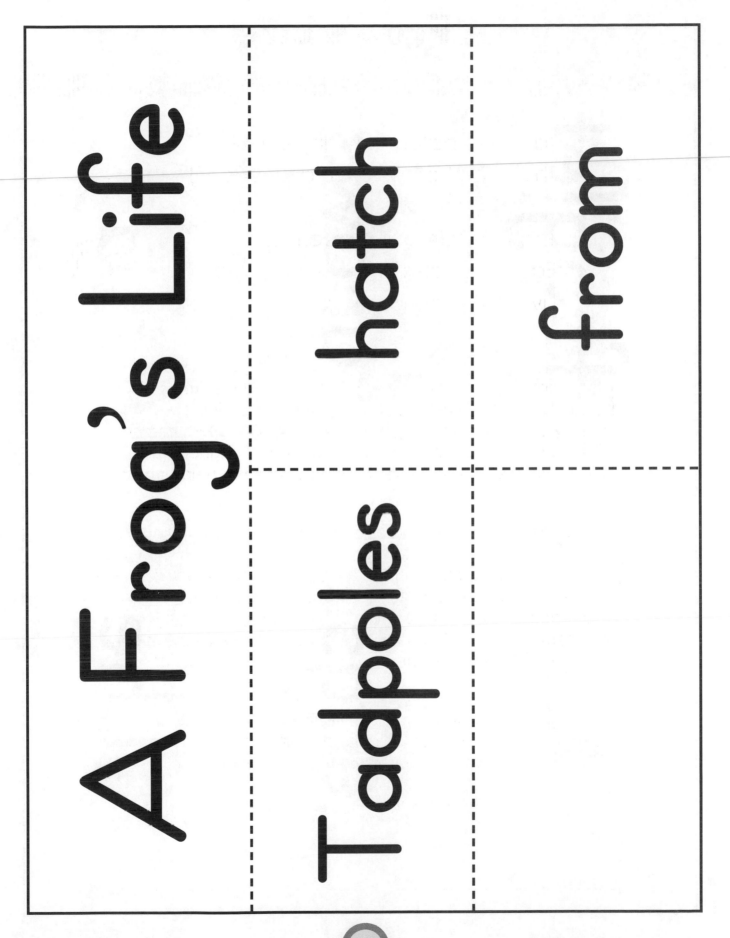

A Frog's Life

hatch

from

Tadpoles

froglet

grows

a

tiny

eggs.

The

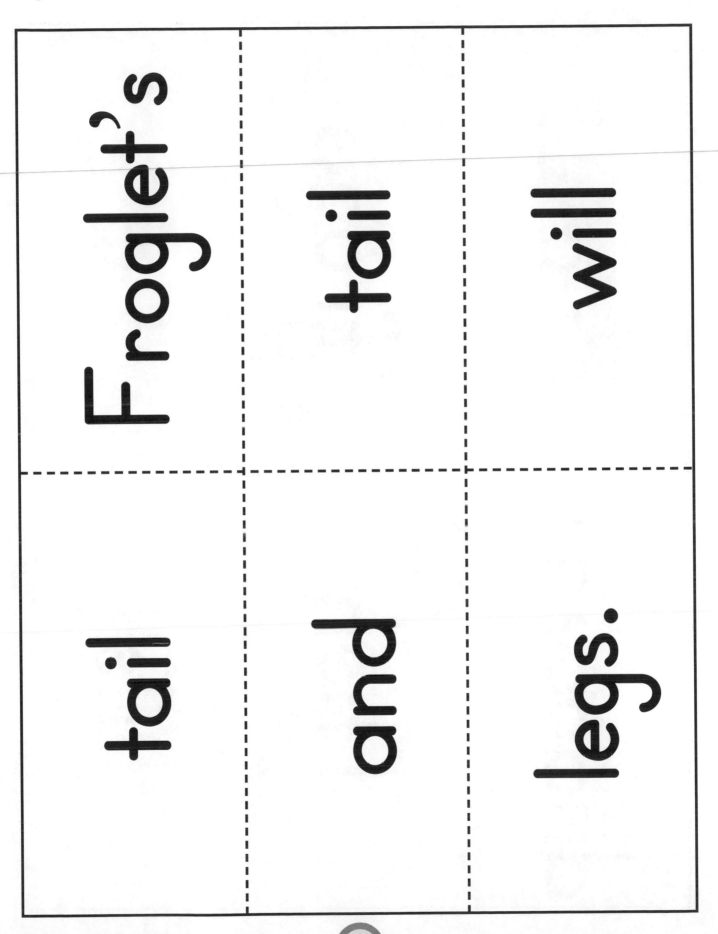

Froglet's

tail

will

tail

and

legs.

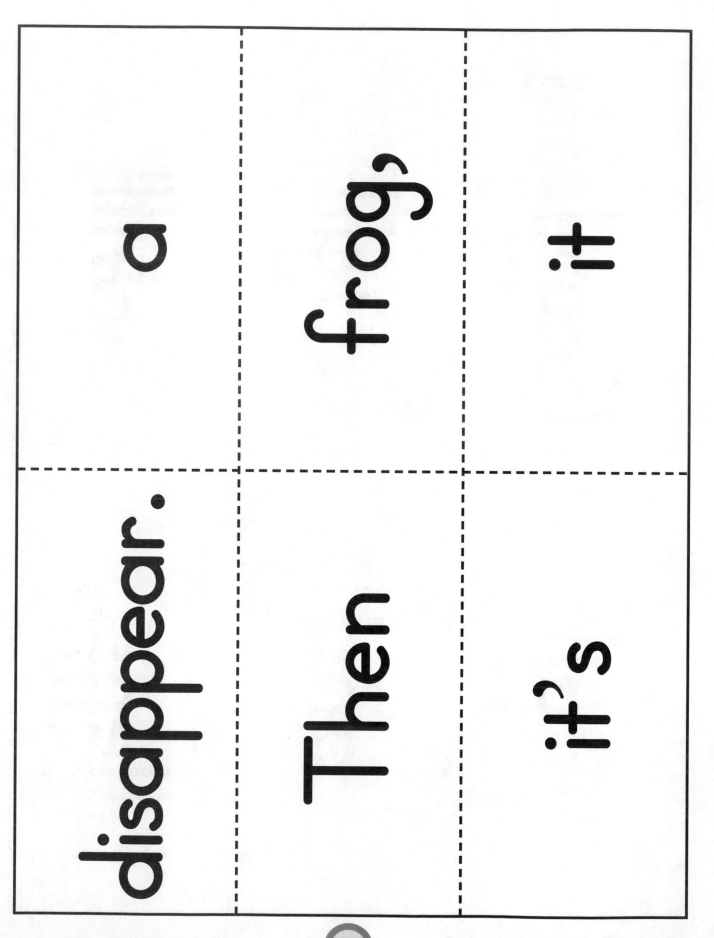

a

frog,

it

disappear.

Then

it's

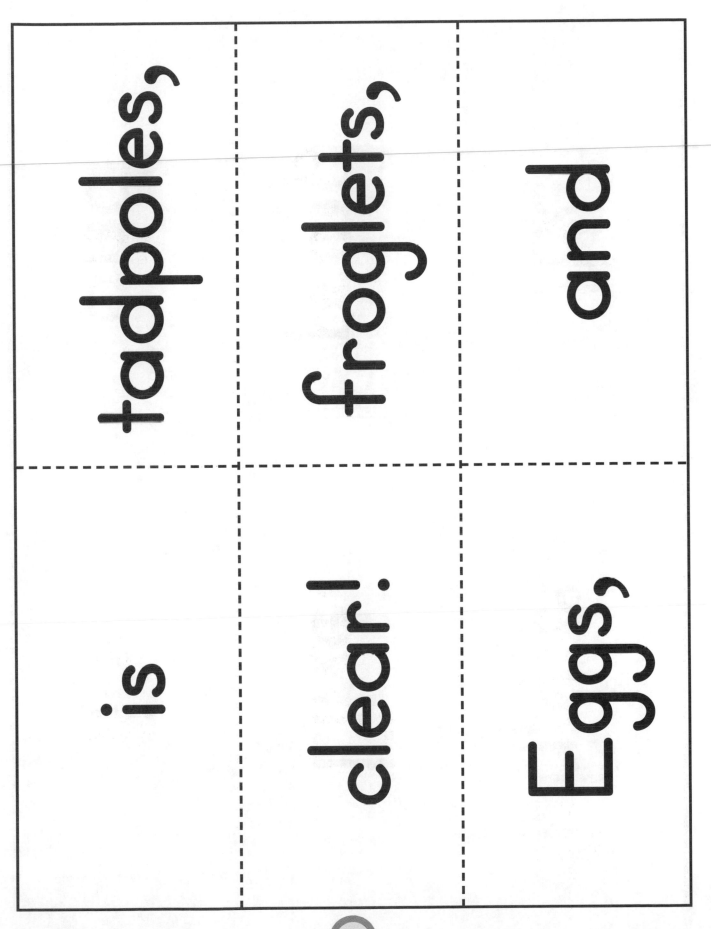

tadpoles,

froglets,

and

is

clear!

Eggs,

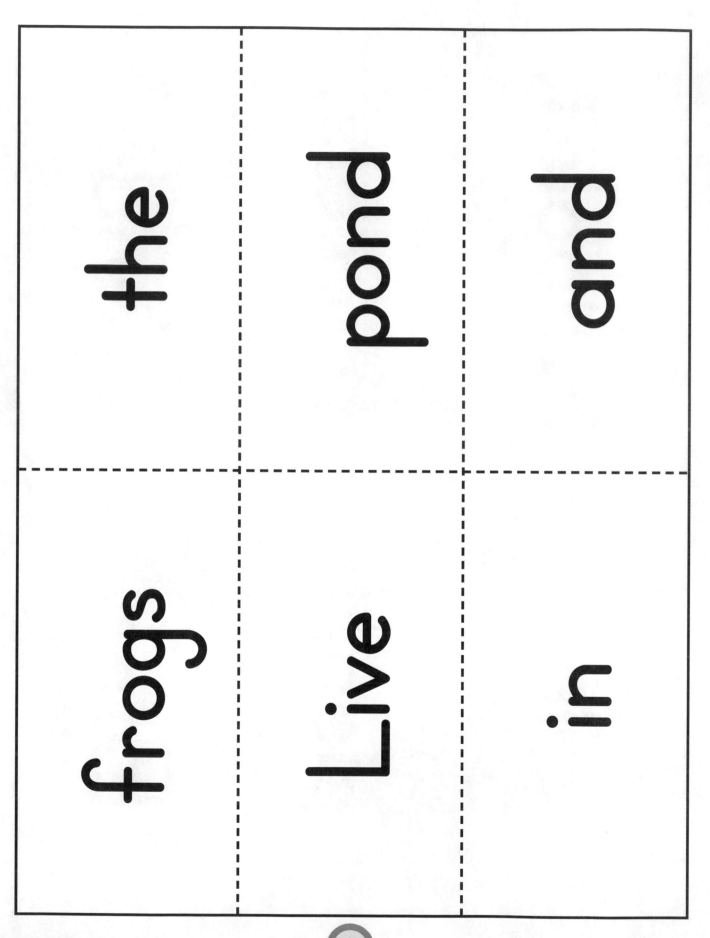

the

pond

and

frogs

Live

in

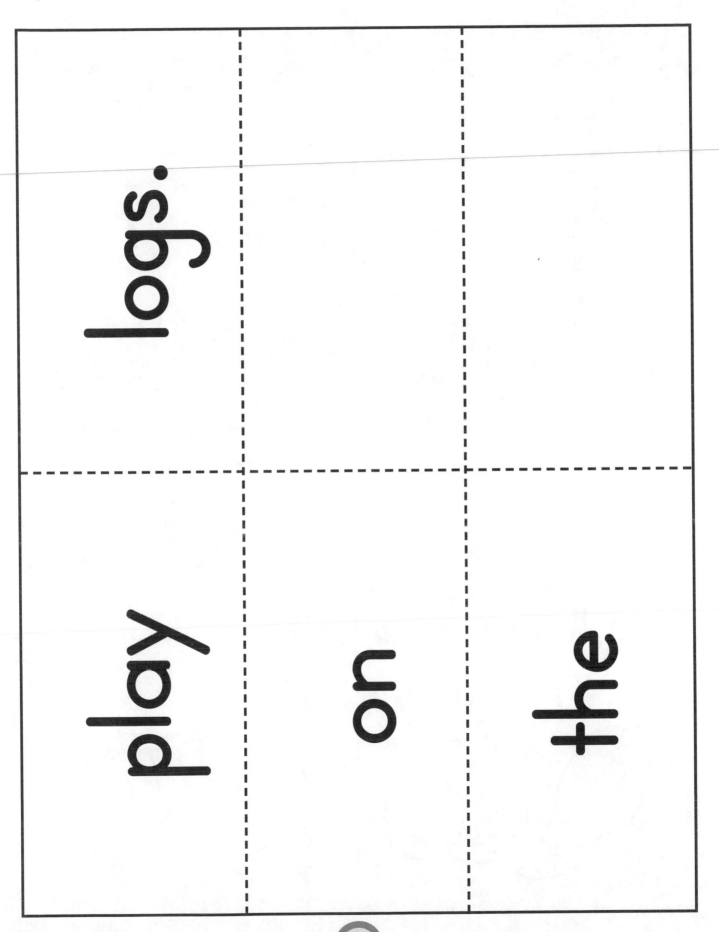

logs.

play

on

the

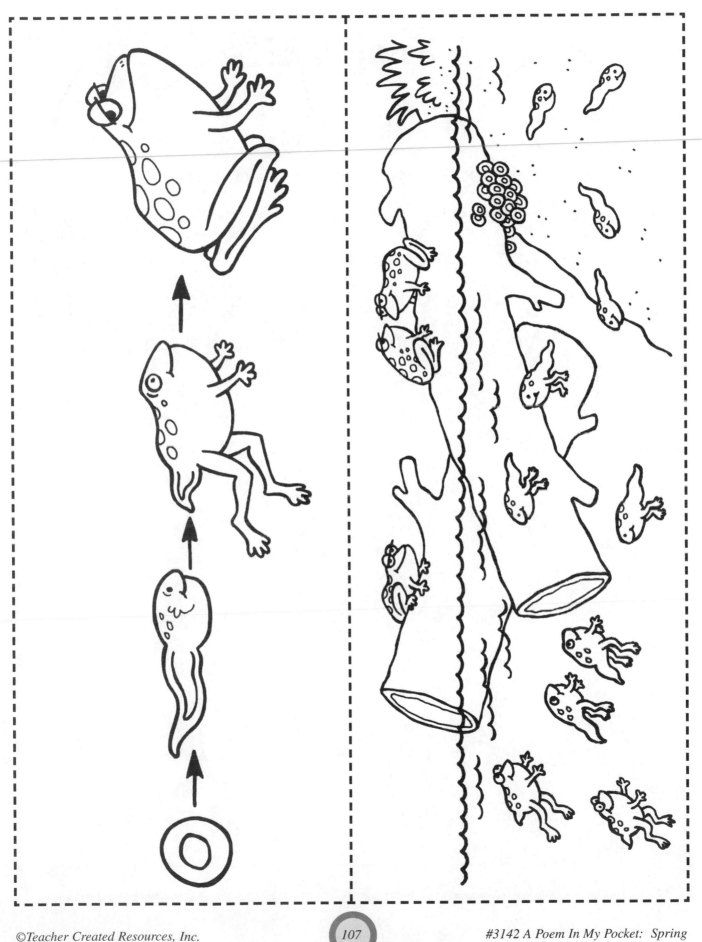

A Frog's Life

Tadpoles hatch from tiny eggs.
The froglet grows a tail and legs.
Froglet's tail will disappear.
Then it's a frog, it is clear!
Eggs, tadpoles, froglets, and frogs
Live in the pond and play on the logs.

I like _____!

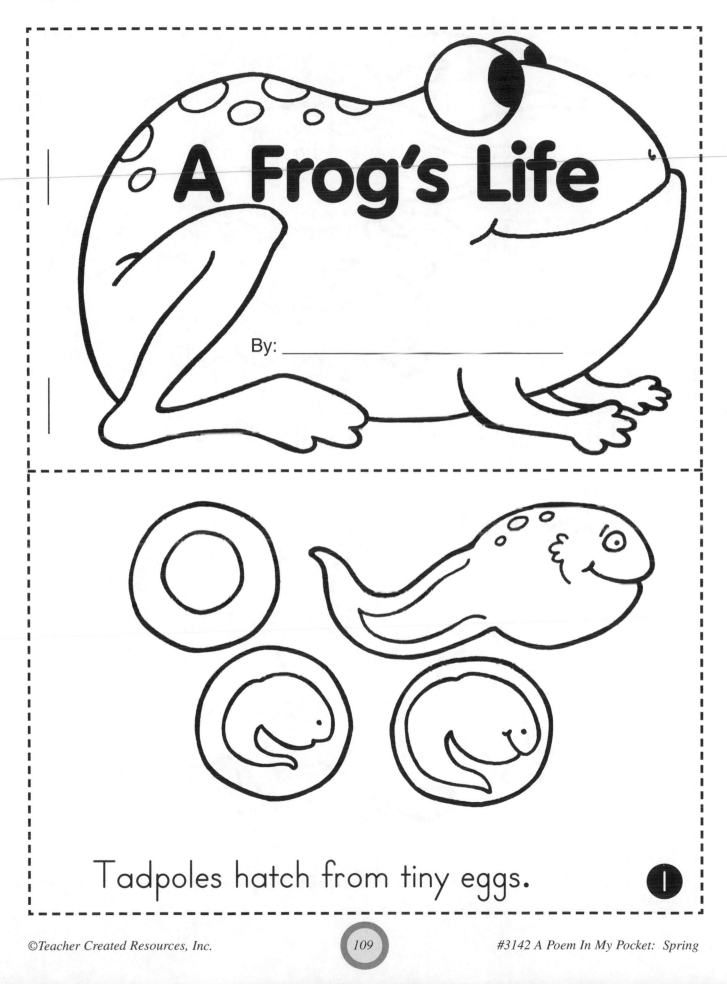

A Frog's Life

By: _____

Tadpoles hatch from tiny eggs.

1

The froglet grows a tail and legs. **2**

Froglet's tail will disappear. **3**

Then it's a frog, it is clear! **4**

Eggs, tadpoles, froglets, and frogs **5**

Live in the pond and play
on the logs.   **6**

Ff

Find all the words that start with the
letter **f** and underline them.   **7**